D1490979

F#CK CONTENT MARKETING

F#CK CONTENT MARKETING

MARKETING

FOCUS ON CONTENT EXPERIENCE TO DRIVE DEMAND, REVENUE & RELATIONSHIPS

RANDY FRISCH

LIONCREST
PUBLISHING

COPYRIGHT © 2019 RANDY FRISCH
All rights reserved.

F#CK CONTENT MARKETING
Focus on Content Experience to Drive
Demand, Revenue & Relationships

ISBN   978-1-5445-1365-2 *Hardcover*
      978-1-5445-1364-5 *Paperback*
      978-1-5445-1363-8 *Ebook*
      978-1-5445-1366-9 *Audiobook*

CONTENTS

_____

FOREWORD

BY JON MILLER

My whole career has been dedicated to pursuing the vision of a book called *The One to One Future*, by Don Peppers and Martha Rogers, PhD. Around the time that book dropped, I was headed for an advanced degree in physics at MIT, but suddenly, I decided I wanted to give the business world a try. So, I got a job at a management consulting firm, where I learned how to use data and analytics to help make better customer systems. I fell in love with this world and began dreaming of ways to turbocharge these systems to personalize at scale.

That's about the time I discovered *The One to One Future*. The central vision of that book is the idea of the 1800s corner store. From the moment you walked in, the storekeepers knew everything about you—whether you preferred brown eggs to white eggs, whether you needed an extra bag of flour because your family was visiting next week. Because they knew *you*, they always knew exactly what you needed. Then, the Industrial Revolution took hold, bringing with it mass production and economies of scale. Sure, customers got greater choice and lower prices, but those benefits came at a cost: we lost that one-to-one level of personalization and relevance.

If things stopped there, we might interpret that as rather bleak. But the authors assure us there's hope. Using data and analytics, we can effectively deliver that corner-store-level of personalization at industrial-era scale. That idea has been the inspiration for my entire career.

Some of you reading this may know my resume. First, I spent some time at a company called Epiphany, a leading marketing platform in the late nineties that popped with the internet bubble some time later. After selling the company in 2005, along with Phil Fernandez, I started a company called Marketo (which, as I write this, was recently acquired by Adobe for a cool $4.75 billion). These days, I've helped found a company called Engagio. With all of my companies, the goal is always the same: try to get close to delivering on the vision of *The One to One Future*.

In the service of that goal, I've been at the center of

many hot marketing trends. Marketo was one of the first modern companies to use content to build and define a brand, and we helped define the category of marketing automation. More recently, my work at Engagio has put us at the forefront of a category called Account Based Marketing (ABM), and we've used content (such as our Clear and Complete Guide to Account Based Marketing) to establish ourselves as thought leaders. So, it goes without saying that I am a passionate believer in the power and value of content marketing.

Now, at this point you may be wondering, why did the author of a book called *F#ck Content Marketing* ask one of content marketing's biggest fans to write the foreword? I'll let Randy tell you how he arrived at that title in his own words, but here's the short version: it's not the content itself that this book is rallying against, but rather the lack of support that content receives from the rest of the marketing team.

I get it. My core belief in content comes from a belief that marketing should be loved. Unfortunately, given the state of marketing today, most consumers don't feel that way, avoiding marketing wherever they can. We have ad skippers and blockers on our browsers. We gleefully hit the spam button on unwanted marketing messages. We mute the TV and pull out our smartphones during every commercial break. The dominant narrative is—and has been—that marketing is bad and should be avoided.

Basic economic theory would disagree. If somebody buys your product, they are saying that they consider your product or service more valuable than the money they're giving you. Otherwise, they wouldn't buy it. When we marketers help facilitate a transaction, then we're helping people find products and services that are valuable to them, and in turn, we are creating economic value. We're creating good in the world. From that perspective, everybody should love marketing, and yet, it's painfully obvious that they don't. Why? Too often, marketing is purely promotional and not about delivering value to the recipient.

That's why I love content—it's all about delivering value. Content is educational. Content is entertaining. Content is useful. That's why I went hard into content, and why I think other marketers did as well. Especially in the B2B world, content helps build trusted brands—which matters since trust is critical when a complex B2B purchase can mean the difference between someone getting promoted or losing their job.

This isn't to say that content is above criticism, of course. Someone once said that marketers will flock to any successful tactic until they kill it. In my experience, that sentiment is absolutely true—and I fear that it's happened to content. In the early days of Marketo, using content to build a brand was a novel, albeit successful, idea. These days, everybody and their mom is a content producer. We're all suffering from content overload.

To be clear, content is still important, especially in the B2B world. According to the IT Services Marketing Association, 75 percent of executives said that they would respond to an unsolicited marketing outreach if it contained ideas that were "meaningful and relevant" to their business. To accomplish relevance, content should feel as though:

1. It was tailored to their specific industry.
2. It was tailored to the unique needs and challenges of their business.
3. It contained ideas that could help them move their business forward.

We try to avoid most of the crap that comes our way, but as soon as we know something is actually meaningful and relevant, we embrace it because it helps us do our jobs.

So relevance matters—a lot. But in today's noisy environment, relevance is necessary but not sufficient for success. The real question is, as marketers, how do we get that meaningful and relevant content *in front of* the people who need to see it?

The answer begins with personalization. In *The Challenger Sale*, authors Matthew Dixon and Brent Adamson found that the best, most successful sales people personalize every customer experience. Not only do they teach their customers as part of the sales process, but they also tailor their lessons to account for the specific business. I don't know about you, but that sounds a lot like personalized content marketing to me.

That's the promise that drew me to this book as well. I've known Randy since he co-founded Uberflip and later started to advocate for content experience. It became clear after our first coffee at Mimi's Cafe in San Mateo that he saw the same problems with content marketing that I do, and that a focus on content experience could be the solution. The focus needs to evolve away from simply creating content and toward ensuring that content finds that right person at the right time and in the right context—in other words, that it's personalized and valuable to the person receiving it. This book has all the tips you need to bring the vision of *The One to One Future*—corner-store-level personalization at industrial-era scale—to your own organization.

Jon is a marketing entrepreneur and thought leader. He was a cofounder at Marketo, a leader in marketing automation later purchased by Adobe for $4.75 billion. Jon is currently the CEO and cofounder of Engagio, a platform that orchestrates ABM.

DISCLAIMER

WE LOVE CONTENT MARKETERS (SERIOUSLY!)

—

Don't let the title of this book fool you. We love content marketing—and we love our content marketers even more. However, before you read any further, I want to be perfectly clear on a few points:

- This is not a book about content marketing.
- This is not a book about how to create great content—or how to create any content, for that matter.
- This is not a book written for content marketers, though if you are a content marketer, you'll love this book because (a) we have your back, and (b) it will give your organization perspective of what needs to happen after you click publish.

So, what is this book about, and who is it for?

- If you're working in the marketing department in roles like demand generation, digital marketing, or account-based marketing (and of course content marketing), this book is for you.
- If you're working in other departments within your organization—in sales, HR, even accounts receivable—this book is for you, too.
- If you use content in any way in the process of doing your job, this book is for you.

Whether we're shooting off emails, crafting training videos for new hires, or even putting together an invoice, we all need good content. And wherever there's content, there's an experience. The more intentional you are in creating that experience, the better you'll connect with your audience.

If you're interested in learning more about the content experience and what it can do for your marketing efforts, read on.

LET ME EXPLAIN MYSELF

WHAT THE F#CK IS UP WITH THIS BOOK TITLE?

———

I was sitting on the plane, waiting to head out to Salesforce's annual Dreamforce Conference, a big sales and marketing event that draws professionals from every industry. As our plane sat on the tarmac, I was browsing around on my smartphone when I came across a stat courtesy of SiriusDecisions that I couldn't believe was real:

Sixty to seventy percent of all marketing content goes unused.[1]

---

1   It's worth noting that this statistic applies specifically to B2B marketers. For more information, see: Jessica Lillian, "Summit 2013 Highlights: Inciting a B-to-B Content Revolution." *SiriusDecisions*. May 9, 2013. https://www.siriusdecisions.com/blog/summit-2013-highlights-inciting-a-btob-content-revolution

Talk about a scary number.

For years, marketing leaders have been investing in content marketing nonstop. The commonly accepted idea is that the more content you produce, the more you attract the attention of your target audience, and the more customers or clients you convert. But this data had just flipped that notion on its head. If most of the content we were producing was going unused, what was the point of creating it at all?

These thoughts had been crawling around my head long before I read that stat. The number just made the problem more real. At any rate, despite my concerns, I too had been relentlessly banging the content marketing drum the past few years. Anyone on my content team was used to hearing me running around the office asking for more content:

> "We don't have enough new posts this week. What's up with that?"

> "Why haven't we put out any ebooks lately?"

> "Where's that podcast you promised we were going to launch?"

Our audience had to know we were still out there adding

value, so every week, I pushed our team to make X number of easy-to-consume posts on channels A, B, and C, come hell or high water. When I read that stat, however, it reminded me to hit the pause button and listen to what my inner voice was telling me: something had to change.

Now that I had some real numbers to help me give voice to my concerns—and free from all distractions on a flight without Wi-Fi—I had my Jerry Maguire moment. It was time to write my mission statement (not a memo!). By the time the plane touched down, I'd written a long, passionate blog post (even as the CMO, I still write blog posts) with a blinding title: "F#ck Content Marketing."

This wasn't the first time I'd written an epically long blog post during a Wi-Fi-free flight. In fact, by that time, my team at Uberflip had come to expect the occasional several-thousand-word post. Usually, I'd send it off, and a few hours later, they'd reply with some gentle ribbing—"Oh, where were you flying to this time, Randy?" or "What, there weren't any good in-flight movies to watch?"

This time, however, there was none of that. As soon as I sent the post off, my team shot me an urgent reply: "There is absolutely no way we're going to let you publish this."

"Hear me out," I replied. "At least dig into this one a little bit before you reject it. I need you to understand what I'm trying to say."

I had their attention. Now I just had to convince them.

WHEN CONTENT MARKETING GOT F#CKED

From the moment it first became a buzzword, marketing leaders began the mad scramble to quantify and define the concept of content marketing. My favorite definition came courtesy of Joe Pulizzi and Robert Rose at the Content Marketing Institute (CMI), whose work more than anyone else's helped marketers to understand the value of creating content:

> Content marketing is a marketing technique of creating and distributing valuable, relevant, and consistent content to attract and acquire a clearly defined audience—with the objective of driving profitable customer action.

For Pulizzi and Rose, content marketing wasn't just about creating content, but also about *attracting an audience.* Over time, despite their advocacy for a holistic view, their message became distorted. CMOs began putting all their budget and focus into content creation, all but ignoring what happens to that content after—and whether it is, in fact, working to attract an audience. It was like a game of broken telephone, with the message—and value—of content marketing being obscured in the process. Ultimately, two key factors contributed to this unfortunate reality.

#1: UNCLEAR JOB DESCRIPTIONS

When CMI first put out their definition of content marketing, brands took one look at it and said, "Well, if we're going to create something that bonds with our audience, we're going to need content—and lots of it." The question was, who was going to create all that content? Naturally, the content marketer!

Unsure of where else to turn, these brands went out, hired a bunch of eager young journalists and storytellers, and told them to start producing content. It was a good start, but ultimately a flawed one. For one, these content marketers may have had a mandate, but they had little to no guidance or support from the organizations who hired them. Even today, if you go to LinkedIn, Glassdoor, or any other of the many recruiting sites out there, the job descriptions for "content marketer" all look about the same, with each describing a role that is almost exclusively focused on producing content. Very rarely do these descriptions go beyond content creation, and for good reason: they *shouldn't*. Content creation is a full-time job, not something you squeeze out in between other tasks. (Even writing a book like this one creates zoning in for long stretches.) Unfortunately, many organizations don't see it that way, loading their content marketers up with a whole range of other tasks—managing the content life cycle, attracting an audience, and guiding them through the buyer's journey, converting prospects into customers, and so on. I'm not saying one person doesn't have all these skill sets, I know many content marketers who do, but the question is, should they be expected to balance this all?

It doesn't take an organizational expert to understand that this is a less-than-ideal scenario. When you fail to support your content marketers and push them to complete tasks for which they have very little expertise or bandwidth, just about everybody loses—the brand, the content marketer, and the audience.

#2: CMP CONFUSION

While all these organizations were snapping up journalists left and right and converting them into content marketers, a tsunami of software companies rose up from the ocean, each offering solutions for streamlining the content marketing process. "We are a content marketing platform (CMP). You can't create and distribute content without us," they boldly declared, and organizations accepted what they were selling, no questions asked.

To be fair, this isn't to say that platforms like NewsCred,

Kapost, or Contently aren't or weren't valuable. It's just that they only solved for half of the content marketing equation: create the content. The other heaping half of the equation—packaging and distributing the content at scale—was largely ignored. As a result, the promise of content marketing as first envisioned by CMI went only half-fulfilled, and brands everywhere were forced to settle for an approach that stressed content creation and all but ignored the crucial next step of audience engagement.

THE F-BOMB HEARD 'ROUND THE MARKETING WORLD

This was the argument I laid out in my blog post—and the one I made again as I begged my content team to publish it. As I saw it, the promise of content marketing had yet to be fulfilled. Sure, (some) brands were great at creating content, but by and large, they sucked at mapping that content to the buyer's journey or other measurable outcomes.

As I explained how content marketing had gone wrong and my dilemma over process and terminology, I realized I had a choice to make. I could rally against it, or just let it be and accept that content marketing, as practiced today, is about creating content—nothing more, nothing less. I chose the latter. It was best for everyone if I waved the white flag and left content marketing to the creators.

My conclusion, however, was that I was unwilling to surrender.

If we're just making content for the sake of making content, then f#ck it.

If we're going to waste 60-70 percent of our content marketers' hard work, then f#ck it.

If we're not going to fulfill the promise of content marketing, then f#ck it—and f#ck content marketing.

Just as I was working myself up into a frenzy and running out of creative ways to drop F-bombs, my team slowly started to come around.

"You know what?" one of them said. "I actually kind of agree with you now. F#ck my job if all the content I created is going to go unused. What's the point of me sweating over creating all this stuff if no one sees it?"

Finally, they understood. I didn't write that post—and now this book—to throw content marketers under the bus. Quite the opposite—I think content marketers are often undervalued. I wrote them as a way of *jumping behind* content marketers everywhere and giving them the support they deserve.

Now that I'd earned their permission to publish that post, only one question remained: did I really have to use the F-bomb?

Okay, maybe I didn't have to, but none of the other alternatives hit the mark in quite the same way. "Stop content marketing" was misleading. We didn't want anyone to stop or slow down their content output. "Screw content marketing" was softer, but it also lost something in the translation—and in some ways, it felt more hostile than I'd intended it. "What's the point of content marketing?" was just cumbersome and awful. We tossed that option out as quickly as it was suggested.

Suggestion after suggestion was floated by one person or another, but no substitution proved as versatile, nuanced, and, yes, eye-catching as a good old-fashioned F-bomb. Somehow, I'd have to explain to my three kids that I wrote a book and the title wasn't quite as soft as *Goodnight Moon*. Anyway, we weren't saying "f#ck content marketing" as a way of dismissing it, but rather as a way of supporting it, and I was willing to bet that other marketers would understand exactly what I meant.

WHY YOU SHOULD SAY "F#CK CONTENT MARKETING" TOO

Admit it: if you're the CMO or the CEO of your company, you've probably thought of saying, "F#ck content marketing!" once or twice yourself. And why shouldn't you? So much of your budget has gone toward creating content, toward investing in an abundance of software, and toward countless hours of head scratching as you try to get that content in front of your audience. Content marketing has long been hailed as the great fix-all of the digital age, and yet, you're just not seeing the returns you think you should.

The good news is, if you're investing in content marketing, you *are* on the right path. Today, most CEOs have bought into the idea of content marketing and understand its value, which is why, every year, about 70 percent of B2B marketers expect they will create more content (similar numbers exist for B2C).[2] But as the Gartner Hype Cycle teaches us, sometimes the process of buying in alone leads to inflated expectations. Whether it's email, social media, wearables, artificial intelligence, or, yes, content marketing, whatever new trend over the years we hitch our wagons to, we expect it to lead the way to revenue.

When we inevitably realize that isn't the case, we quickly plummet from our idealistic perch and become deeply and terribly disillusioned. "Holy sh#t," we say, "this isn't as easy as I thought. It turns out I can't just write a blog

---

2   Joe Pulizzi and Ann Handley, B2B Content Marketing: 2017 Benchmarks, Budgets, and Trends—North America, Content Marketing Institute and MarketingProfs: 2017, https://contentmarketinginstitute.com/wp-content/uploads/2016/09/2017_B2B_Research_FINAL.pdf.

or start a podcast and expect my audience to find it. This content marketing thing is actually going to require some serious effort."

It sure is. But done right, it's also incredibly worth it.

So, if you've reached this point with content marketing, right now you have a choice. Throw your hands up, say "F#ck it," and walk away, or dig in and actually think about when and how your content can help you win.

WELCOME TO THE CONTENT EXPERIENCE

Content marketing has served us well over the past decade or so. Today, however, more and more organizations are realizing that's not enough. Content alone isn't some magic cure-all. This isn't *Field of Dreams* where if you build it, they will come. Here, once you have it, you have to *use it*. And to do that, you and everyone in your organization must join together to say, "F#ck content marketing!" and then turn your focus to what we call *content experience.*

So, what exactly is content experience? At my company, Uberflip, we define content experience in the following way:

A content experience is (1) the **environment** in which

your content lives, (2) how it's **structured**, and (3) how it compels your prospects and customers to **engage** with your company.

Ultimately, mastering the content experience involves three elements:

1. A strategic approach toward creating the environment in which your audience consumes your content.
2. Structuring your content for easy discoverability within that environment.
3. Encouraging your audience to engage with you—and ultimately convert—as you lead them through the buyer's journey.

In our day-to-day as consumers, brands like Spotify, Amazon, and Netflix have understood the value of experience for years, masterfully shaping how we as consumers enjoy our "content." In the B2B world, however, we tend to think that what works in the B2C world doesn't apply to us. That couldn't be further from the truth. In fact, according to Salesforce, 82 percent of B2B purchasers expect the same level of personalization in B2B environments that they get in their consumer world.[3] (It makes me laugh to think what the other 20 percent of buyers expect.) I try not to differentiate between what B2B or

3   Vala Afshar. "New Research Uncovers Big Shifts in Customer Expectations and Trust." *Salesforce,* 2018, https://www.salesforce.com/blog/2018/06/digital-customers-research.html

B2C would do and focus on what it takes to close a complex or considered purchase. Either way, you can't tell me that personalization wouldn't be a key factor in the time to close a sale and customer loyalty. With the framework outlined in this book, here is your chance to deliver on that expectation, providing your target buyers with the content they need when they need it.

BEGINNING THE CONTENT EXPERIENCE JOURNEY

It's probably not a great thing to say to start off a book, but here's the truth: I'm not the biggest book guy. Like many readers, I don't finish many of the books I start. Every now and then, though, I pick up a book that I can't put down. Then, once I'm done with it, I immediately set out to find someone else I can pass the book along to so it can change their life as well.

Naturally, I'd love it if this were one of those books that you can't put down, that changes the way you see marketing and your role within it (even if you're not on the marketing team), and that inspires you to share it with others. If you're just in it for a few chapters and some good lessons, that's okay, too. You'll get value from the experience either way.

To make things as easy-to-follow as possible, I've divided this book into three parts:

- **In Part I**, we'll start by taking a look at what's going on in the consumer world, dissecting the approaches that make brands like Spotify and Disney so successful at creating immersive experiences. Then, we'll look at how to apply those tactics as marketers to create an immersive content experience—whether our go-to-market strategy is inbound, demand generation, account-based marketing (ABM), or sales enablement.

- **In Part II**, if I've managed to hook you into the idea of content experience and you want to know how to scale content experience within your organization, I'll walk you through our Content Experience Framework, step by step. Don't worry, I'll try to make this as anti-textbooky as possible. No going into the weeds here—just a nice, solid approach designed to help you execute.

- **In Part III**, we'll talk about how you can rally your entire organization around content experience, helping to unite your messaging and carry your buyers and customers through a journey.

Finally, at the end of the book, you'll hear from my partner in crime, Uberflip co-founder Yoav Schwartz, who will offer you a look to the future of content and the content experience. Throughout the years, Yoav and I have always had each other's backs—me, the marketer with a thousand ideas struggling to find the perfect software platform, and Yoav, the user experience expert and product visionary capable of making the lives of marketers like myself (and you) easier so we can actually get sh#t done. Ultimately, this book is the result of that journey and partnership. Important to note: this book doesn't pimp our product, but why we created it.

And so, with all that out of the way, it's time to get started. As you move through the following chapters, always remember these words: if you're not going to use the content you produce, then f#ck content marketing. However, if you're ready to begin leveraging your content to connect with your audience and move them along the buyer's journey, then it's time to focus on content experience.

PART I

STATE OF THE UNION

Today, a huge percentage of us relies on Netflix to binge on content we all love. We do it without a second thought. I even look forward to receiving Netflix's weekly emails telling me about new content. Similarly, I love using Spotify to find out about artists I would have never listened to on my own. And several times a week, I browse Amazon not just for things I need, but also just because I'm curious.

The important thing is, whether I'm streaming videos and music or I'm shopping online, I'm not overwhelmed by the many, many options in front of me. Why? Because these sites make it easy to find what I'm looking for, even recommending content and products to me based on my tastes and past habits.

For the purposes of this book, let's call these "Made For You" personalized experiences (I'll tell you where I got this term soon). I've gotten used to these personalized experiences. We all have. I expect that kind of treatment from the consumer brands I interact with. That's not always the case in the B2B world. Too often, B2B brands expect me to take too many steps to find the content I want. They may have great content, but that great content comes with a sh#tty experience. That's got to change.

Over the last ten years, B2B marketers have just started to come around to the idea of putting the right content out there to attract audiences. The holy grail solution to all was email automation. If you could zone in on your target buyer with a drip of emails, that would be enough, right? You'd say, "Okay, we've zoned in on our audience, who are young people between the ages of twenty and twenty-five living on the East Coast and looking for the exact kind of product we offer." Then, you'd target that demographic and drop all of them into the same generic email nurture campaign, or direct mail package, and hope that a certain percentage of them would make it down the sales funnel.

The segmentation was great, but for most marketers, the attention to detail stopped there. But it shouldn't. At every stage of the buyer's journey, we should be asking ourselves: Can we be doing more to personalize the experience with our prospective customers? How do we create a customer experience that delivers the right content at the right time?

How are we going to *engage* our audience and make them feel valued?

Content can help here. No matter your go-to-market strategy, whether it's inbound, demand generation, account-based marketing, or sales enablement, content can extend the Made For You experience.

In Part I, that's what we're going to explore.

CHAPTER 1

WE CRAVE A PERSONALIZED EXPERIENCE

———

Do you remember the way we used to consume music?

When I was twelve years old, if I had a crush on a girl, I would put together a mixtape for her. While they're a little dated today, mixtapes are a perfect example of a personalized experience. In fact, sometimes they were maybe a little too personalized. I remember obsessing over which twelve or so songs would go on each side.

Making a mixtape was a big undertaking. Unless you had endless amounts of free time, you couldn't just churn out a new one each day. That's what made them such perfect tokens of affection for our crushes. When you made a mixtape for someone, you were telling that person how important they were to you.

Our listening habits—how we experience and consume music—have changed a lot since then. Now, we live in an age where we can find whatever music we're looking for in an instant, and that music can be tailored to our mood, the time of day, or our recent browsing habits. As mentioned, we used to be limited to about twenty-four songs per mixtape. Now I can make playlists on Spotify (or sub your preferred service) with as many tracks as I want.

My son Ethan, for instance, has a playlist called "The #1 Playlist of All Time," which, last time I checked, has over 584 songs on it. While the twenty-four songs I selected for my mixtapes were set once I recorded them, Ethan's playlist is fluid. Sometimes he'll add some tracks, and sometimes he'll delete some. It all depends on the experience he's looking for in that moment.

This extreme personalization comes in handy when, for instance, my son and I are on the road headed to a hockey tournament. He'll open Spotify, assume the role of DJ, and start selecting whatever tracks he feels suit our mood. On the way to the tournament, he'll select upbeat music that hypes him up for the game. On the way home, he's all about finding tracks that will help us wind down. The beauty of Spotify is that he doesn't need to know the specific songs he's interested in ahead of time; he can simply pull up the "mood" section, specify what he's looking for, and Spotify takes care of the rest.

In fact, Spotify has become so sophisticated that it now creates daily playlists for its users that match their usual activities and habits. If you always listen to funk and soul at 10 a.m., for instance, Spotify knows this, and they'll curate a new playlist of funk and soul jams for your mid-morning break.

Imagine if we could have created the same level of personalization—on a daily basis—for our crushes when we made them mixtapes back in the day. We'd never lose out to the competition again (granted we also didn't have Tinder/Bumble). Back then, though, putting together a mixtape was impressive enough. Today, especially in the consumer world, expectations for a personalized experience are much, much higher.

LEADING YOUR AUDIENCE THROUGH THE BUYER JOURNEY

Every year, Mary Meeker from Kleiner Perkins comes up with a report on top internet trends. In her 2018 report, Meeker examined personalization, specifically through the lens of Spotify and how it drives customer satisfaction. Over a three-year period (2014–2017), a couple of stats grew dramatically and caught my attention. Spotify's daily engagement went up from 37 percent to 44 percent. *Interesting,* I thought, *but why?* Here's the part that really caught me: In 2014, people were listening to an average of 68 unique artists per month. By 2017, the number grew to 112 different artists every month.[4] I mean, music hasn't gotten better in recent years (debatable, but for another book).

As B2B marketers, what can we learn from the huge amount of growth Spotify has been able to achieve? Simply put, Spotify has taken personalization to the next level. Rather than just taking user data and using that to play the same music they know their listeners love ad nauseam, they use that data to introduce their listeners to new ideas.

In the content game, this is how we have to start thinking about our role as marketers. Often, we find ourselves in the position of selling an idea that our target buyers just aren't ready to discover yet. I can't tell you how often I hear marketers say things like, "I just can't get them to consume the content I need them to." That doesn't mean we can't get them there, of course, but it *does* mean we have to be strategic in how we go about it. Spotify offers

---

4   Mary Meeker, *Internet Trends 2018,* Kleiner Perkins, May 30, 2018, https://www.kleinerperkins.com/perspectives/internet-trends-report-2018/.

an excellent blueprint for guiding your audience through the buyer's journey.

Spotify calls this their "Made For You" feature. Think of it this way. There are (hopefully) thousands of people loving this book. And if every one of us reached into our pocket, pulled out our phone, and opened Spotify, we'd each have a unique Made For You playlist. We'd also discover recommendations for new artists who we didn't know existed. Spotify knows how to hook their listeners in with tried and true content, while slowly introducing other ideas. This is what we're up against as marketers.

Don't sit here and think, "While that's Spotify, my audience doesn't expect that." Let's learn from Spotify and figure out how to deliver personalized content experiences. By embracing a Made For You approach, we can get buyers to discover assets that they may very well fall in love with, leading them to trust and buy.

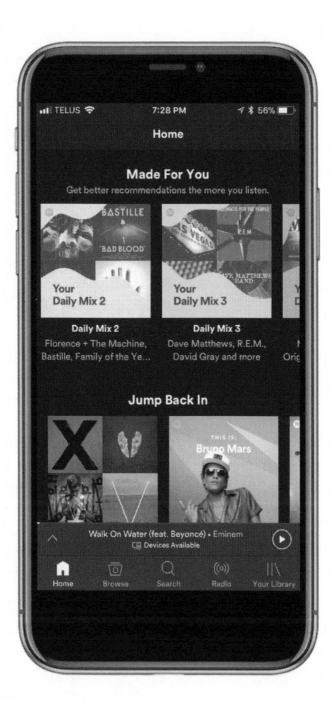

While the Spotify method has proven highly successful, both the B2C and B2B worlds offer many other examples of how to lead your target audience through the buyer's journey. For the rest of this chapter, we're going to look at a few of these approaches more closely, focusing on what makes them so effective (or in some cases, not so effective) in creating a personalized experience worthy of our middle school crushes. At the core of all these approaches is the same guiding principle: use content to keep your target audience engaged with you as you move them along the buyer's journey.

THE INFINITE SCROLL

According to IDG, on average, people need seven pieces of content before they make a buying decision.[5] Our goal as marketers, then, is to serve our audience the right content *at* the right time (whether seven, ten, or, if done right, maybe only three pieces of content) so that we can drive them down the buyer's journey—and do it as efficiently as possible.

In the world of social media, platforms like Instagram, Facebook, and LinkedIn hook us into their content pipeline through what is termed the "infinite scroll." If you're like me, you probably find yourself caught up in

---

5   IDG, 2017 *Customer Engagement Research*, https://www.idg.com/blog/7-steps-to-successful-content-marketing/.

the infinite scroll fairly often. As a regular contributor on LinkedIn, I usually try to spend five minutes or so before bed catching up on my news feed. I open the app, I start to scroll, and before I know it, five, ten, or even twenty minutes or more have gone by. I've been hooked by the infinite scroll, and I'm sure it's happened to you.

What makes the infinite scroll so effective is that the medium presents us with contextual content. When I'm on LinkedIn, I'm not coming across content posted by my friend's sister's therapist, but rather by people who have similar interests to me in the professional sphere. LinkedIn and other social platforms carefully craft our content feeds to keep us moving through, using intelligent algorithms to make sure that we're only seeing the most relevant content from our many connections—and as many of us can attest, it's incredibly effective in locking us into a pattern of consuming content.

The infinite scroll makes consuming content and moving from one piece to the next incredibly easy. It's all built around topics we're interested in, and there are no dead ends. How nice would it be if, as marketers, we could emulate this experience on our own platforms? It's great that our audiences can find our brand on platforms like LinkedIn, Facebook, Instagram, and so on. However, once they've clicked on a piece of our content, what do they do? Usually, they jump right back into the infinite scroll, connecting with other brands and their content when they could be connecting with ours.

We as marketers need to think about the type of scroll we want someone to go through. Too many brands in the B2B world default to a chronological experience—our post on May 13 is followed by our post on May 12, and so on. However, are those two pieces of content relevant or connected in any way? Probably not. The beauty of what platforms like LinkedIn, Facebook, and Instagram are doing is that they learn to adapt and personalize the content for their viewers—and in so doing, continue to keep them on their platform and keep them engaged. Isn't this our goal for owned web properties as marketers?

CAPTIVATED BY THE EXPERIENCE

What is it that makes Disney World so much more magical than most other parks? I'm a huge Disney World fan, but if I'm being honest, their rides aren't the best out there. However, while some niche amusement parks or experiences may have better rides, Disney has mastered the art of guiding us through one experience to the next.

Take Space Mountain. It's okay, as far as roller coasters go. What makes it special is the whole process. From the moment you get in line, they immerse you in the experience, hitting you with nonstop magical moments that keep you entertained, creating a fictional world for your "space adventure." Before you know it, you're off the ride, but the experience continues—right into a gift shop so they can monetize whatever high you might be experiencing from the ride.

Space Mountain is just one example. The beauty of Disney World is that every feature of the park is designed with the user experience (UX) in mind. "Cast members" walking down the streets are everywhere waiting to connect and brighten your day. Couple that with fireworks, parades, and other pop-up performances, everything comes together to keep you engaged and moving through the journey.

While it would be easy to say that what works for a Disney theme park probably isn't going to work for your brand, keep in mind that IKEA does the same kind of thing. IKEA's furniture isn't particularly great. It's not terrible, either, but what keeps us going back and buying items we can't pronounce is that they make the experience and everything surrounding it so easy to understand. A walk through IKEA is literally a walk through specific rooms with specific designs so we can see how all their furniture comes together. They make it easy for us to imagine how we could implement these items in our own space in a way that might have been difficult to do otherwise.

This is what we have to do as marketers. It's not just

about delivering one great ride or building an amazing sofa. It's about how we pull it all together to guide someone through an experience that feels natural. Once the customer buys into the journey, they'll find themselves immersed and learning more about the content being presented.

WHEN CONTENT COMES TO YOU

Even with the beauty of the infinite scroll, people aren't always seeking out content. In those cases, marketers have to be creative in how we get that content in front of our audience.

A few years ago, I was at a festival with my three kids (Ethan, Lyla, and Ryan) and ran into Volkswagen's experiential marketing campaign where people could hop in a bunch of different cars and play interactive games related to their product line. I wasn't looking to buy, but nevertheless I looked at their SUVs since (a) that's my kind of car, and (b) I have three kids! I gave them my email address and figured that if they were smart, Volkswagen would start me on a drip campaign centered on their line of SUVs. I often do this stuff as a marketer. I embrace seeing if brands will rise to the occasion, knowing I can always unsubscribe.

#Fail. Days later, I did indeed start to receive emails

from Volkswagen, but it was clear they hadn't bothered to learn anything more about me than my email address. I knew this because, while I'd spent the entire time looking at their SUVs, the email campaign was clearly geared around selling me a two-door convertible.

Don't get me wrong; it looked like a super fun car to own. But I have three kids (who they gave swag to at the festival). My needs are different, and they didn't bother to learn from our interaction. The campaign was trying to connect with me using content, but completely missed the mark around the personalization. They'd had a great opportunity at the festival to understand me as a buyer, and they hadn't taken it.

Now, as marketers, it's easy to want to chalk this experience up to a missed opportunity, shrug our shoulders, and say we'll do better next time. Just remember, though, that those missed opportunities have repercussions. You know what I did after I got that email from Volkswagen? I deleted it. I'll probably delete the next email from them, too—and the one after that, and the one after that, followed by that unsubscribe, leave-me-alone decision. They didn't just miss the mark in that moment. They also turned me off completely to receiving marketing messages of any kind from them.

To stay on this point a little longer, let's take a look at

another example I had with an automaker who knew exactly how to personalize their content experience. While I was out on a skiing trip, I discovered that Tesla was hosting an in-person test drive at the ski resort. Just like my encounter with Volkswagen, the people at Tesla had me fill out my contact information and some basic details about myself. And just like Volkswagen, they followed up with an email.

That's where the similarities end. The amount of detail that Tesla managed to pull into their nurture emails was amazing. The first one alluded to the car I test drove and then followed up with content on the benefits of owning a Tesla. Everything they sent over completely aligned with the experience I'd had at the ski resort and was personalized to me. The sales rep even sent me a personalized email asking about my brother-in-law, whose leg was broken, to see how he was recovering. Experiences like this illustrate why everyone sees Tesla as really f#cking cool. While Volkswagen treated me like a data point, Tesla invested in my experience.

FORGET YOUR AGENDA

When it comes to the personalized world, we need to remember that it's not about *our* agenda. It's about the customer's. Too often we try to make people care about a great piece of content without doing anything to show that we care about *them*.

Let's go back to some of the consumer examples we touched on earlier. When Netflix has a new show or Spotify has a new album, they don't blast every single one of their subscribers to let every single one of them know. They understand that, in order to not be annoying, they have to deliver the right content that matters to right members of their audience.

Companies like Netflix, Spotify, and Tesla aren't blasting everyone with the same content and trying to make them care. Instead, they deliver personalized content that matters to specific segments of their audience.

True personalization begins when we learn to lead less with our own agenda and focus on designing a journey around our audience's interests. That's why mixtapes were so special back in the day—and that's why Spotify is crushing it in the music streaming game.

Now, that doesn't mean that the content we create can't align to our own agenda, but we need to be smart about how we get there. Ultimately, if we're going to encourage our audience to keep moving from one touchpoint to the next, we need to show them that it's worth their time and that we're not treating them like just another data point.

Before we move on to the next chapter, I'd like to wrap up with a note on privacy—a topic I imagine will only increase in importance from the time this book is published. We live in a personalized world. In both B2C and B2B environments, our customers expect us to know who they are, what their needs are, and how they like to be marketed to. However, we're also living in a time where people are raising a lot of legitimate questions regarding their privacy and the confidentiality of their personal information. To that point, we must always make sure we're *earning* our way to having access to their personal information—and that starts by creating a better content experience.

Many brands are already very good at this. When you download an app, for instance, it asks you if it's okay to track your location and activity. They leave it up to us to decide whether we want to give them access, and we make those decisions quickly with a brief subconscious thought on what value might be offered in return.

What brands are finding—and what you've no doubt experienced in your own life—is that we're way more likely to opt in when our experience with a brand feels personalized out of the gate. When Volkswagen showed that they weren't especially concerned with who I was or what kind of car I might be looking for, I wanted nothing else to do with them. There was no way I was going to share any more personal information than I already had. On the flipside, once Tesla showed that they understood exactly who I was and what I was looking for, I was more than happy to share more information with them and continue down a personalized journey (even becoming a customer).

CHAPTER 2

HOW MARKETING STRATEGY IS ADAPTING TO PERSONALIZATION

———

Here's a joke for you: where's the best place to hide something?

Page two of your Google search results.

That joke has been around a long time, and I never get sick of hearing it. However, the punchline is even more exaggerated at this point. Devices like Google Home, Siri, and Alexa are actually making anything past the first search result increasingly obsolete. Why? Any of those options, as well as Google's "I'm feeling lucky" button, always send you to the very first search result.

This really is the new reality. These days when I say "Hey," it's usually followed by "Google." And my expectation is that the reply to my ask is dead-on accuracy. Merging a few analogies in this book, in 2018, I got a brilliant email campaign from Spotify, where they highlighted "Your 2018 Wrapped" and linked me to results of my year. What shocked me was that of the 13,845 minutes of music listened to by the Frisch family, 28 percent of that time was initiated with a voice-activated device like a Google Home, a lot of that probably tied to my nine-year-old daughter Lyla queuing up her next dance motivation.

Spotify Premium

13,845

AND FOR 28% OF THAT TIME, YOUR WERE USING VOICE DEVICE

That's just how it is in the world of personalized search. We rely so much on voice and first-result accuracy that if we want to know how to poach an egg, we trust that Google, Apple, or Amazon can deliver that answer on the first try without us having to search through a bunch of options. We don't want to put in any work learning how to poach eggs. We simply want the answer as quickly as possible.

We've developed a trust of these technologies and brands we interact with—and increasingly, we expect the same degree of personalization with the other brands we interact with. If you don't figure out how to deliver the right content on your site, in emails, and anywhere else a customer might find and engage with you, then you will lose that customer's trust quickly. To earn and maintain our customers' trust, our job is to be like Google—to deliver content that is accurate, relevant, and personalized to our customers.

THERE'S A BETTER WAY: ACKNOWLEDGING BAD HABITS

Were you to ask them, I'm sure most companies would say they'd love to deliver the kind of personalization and marketing that Google is known for. The problem is, in our current approach to content, we've developed some bad habits. Unfortunately, as we'll see, these bad habits are causing us to lose our way. As you read these, don't feel bad; you're likely not the only one. We've all developed at least a few bad habits, often because we haven't had control over content to handle otherwise. In Part II of the book, we'll arm you with a framework to break them.

BAD HABIT #1: GREETING WITH THE LATEST VS. GREATEST CONTENT

Marketers have this idea that they always need to be

pumping out more and more content for their audiences. If this isn't priority number one every single week, if they're not putting out at least five new pieces of inter-related content, then the implication is that they're failing at their jobs.

To manage this steady barrage of content, marketers begin planning out elaborate content editorial calendars that stretch out three, six, nine months, or more. This gives them a good sense of what they're planning to feed their customers, but little sense or memory of what they've already produced—or if it's even relevant to their customers.

If you're like most organizations, the majority of your content is designed to capture people for the very first time. Sure, you may have some subscribers who regularly check in for updates, but the majority of your audience has no idea what came out *yesterday*, let alone six weeks ago.

You can try to connect each piece of content together on your calendar, but that doesn't mean it's still going to be relevant six weeks down the road. The world, your industry, or your customers' personal lives are in a constant state of flux. Some older content will continue to work well, and some of it won't.

Whatever the case may be, remember that with every

piece of content, it doesn't matter if it's six days or six months old. The first time your customer discovers it, it's *new to them*. If each piece of content is interdependent on several others as a result of your content calendar, then your readers are only going to be left feeling lost and confused when they get to it.

I'll give you an example of what I mean. Right now, my boys are really into Transformers. As of this writing, there are six Transformers movies (five in the main series, and one standalone). And while their inclination might have been to watch the most recent one, nothing would have made much sense if they had. They needed to start at the beginning and fall in love with Bumblebee (the yellow one, for nonfans) and the other characters first to see how they progressed.

If I dropped them right into the fifth Transformers movie (*The Last Knight*), they wouldn't have gravitated toward it as much, because they'd have no idea who these characters were and what was actually going on. For my boys and other Transformers fans, the newest piece of content isn't always the best suited for getting them hooked. What they needed was the right content put in front of them at the right time.

Marketers should be approaching their content with this same mentality. Getting people hooked isn't always about new, new, new. It's about using the content you have and focusing on how you can use it to guide your audience through a journey. Let's talk about how, while considering another bad habit.

BAD HABIT #2: ORGANIZING CONTENT BY FORMAT

People are going to come across your company in many ways. They may find you because they're looking for a solution, they're comparing prices against a competitor, or they're trying to deal with a current business challenge. For each of the many ways your audience might choose to engage, you need to be ready with a relevant first piece of content that is best suited to draw them in and lead them to the next relevant piece of unique content.

The path for each of these different journeys will likely be different. As a marketer, it's your job to figure out which pieces of content are needed to guide someone through to a long-term engagement with your brand. Where are those interactions going to happen? What content do you want to present in that instance?

Once you have the idea for a particular piece of content, the next step is thinking about the right format for the asset. Is it better served as a video? A blog post? An ebook? An infographic? Depending on your needs and where you expect to be meeting your customer along their journey, any one (or more) of these formats is acceptable.

Once you've produced that content, how do you organize it on your site? If you're organizing your content the way most brands do, then you're probably sorting them into format buckets. You have one bucket for blog content, one for ebooks, one for infographics, one for videos, and so on.

However, let's be honest: when was the last time you went to someone's website and said, "I'm going to learn about these people by only watching videos," or "I'll be able to learn about this company by reading this ebook"? Probably never, I'm guessing. For 99.9 percent of us, that's not how it works.

Format buckets are counterintuitive to how most people search out content. Let me take you back to the Spotify analogy once again. I don't say: "Play me a song" or "Play me a podcast." I search by mood or genre, or Spotify suggests music based on my past interactions. There's simply no reason to make your customers jump through different buckets in order to find what they want. When we have a problem or a challenge, most of us want content that's relevant to this issue. We don't care what format it is so much as we just want to find an answer to our question.

Organizing digital content effectively is instrumental for

building trust between your brand and your audience. If content can be organized to be more personalized, it will make the user experience seamless and more enjoyable.

No one understood this more than John Cusack's character in *High Fidelity*. Throughout the movie, Cusack is constantly reorganizing his record collection based on a different set of criteria—not alphabetically or by release date, but through categories that were more meaningful to him, such as the year *he* first listened to it, the records that symbolized different relationships, etc. He takes pride in these organizational journeys because it makes the content more meaningful.

With records, Cusack had to do this work by hand, so it was incredibly time-consuming. However, one of the best things about digital content is that we can organize and reorganize our content again and again with tremendous ease—alphabetically, by year, by mood, by previous likes, you name it. It allows variance and a more customizable experience.

The point is, to deliver content in our personalized world, your content needs to be based on the challenges that people deal with on a daily basis. If people can contextualize content in a way that makes sense to them right out of the gate, they will seek out your brand as a trusted authority.

BAD HABIT #3: IGNORING USER EXPERIENCE

For a long time, we were told as content marketers, quality stood above all else (followed in close second by quantity). Success was defined by how well-written the blog post was or how well-produced a video was. Don't get me wrong, quality is incredibly important, but only when the quality conversation takes user experience into account as well. If we ignore how people actually consume the content—and the quality of that experience—we do so at our own peril.

Companies like Netflix and Spotify are world-class not simply because they offer incredible personalization. The user experience on their respective platforms is excellent as well. Both are eye-catching and beautiful. Both seamlessly flow from one piece of content to the next. If all they had was great content, but that great content got stuck in buffering cycles or wasn't particularly mobile-friendly, their customers would be endlessly frustrated.

In your own life, you've probably had to deal with a platform that provided an endlessly frustrating experience. For me, the first sh#tty user experience for content that comes to mind is that of my healthcare provider. They actually offer some great advice, but any time I try to engage with their site and learn more, it quickly becomes a maddening experience, and I usually end up on WebMD instead. Challenges as simple as finding the navigation menu or search bar drive me nuts. Then when I find the search, it's not autofilling my issue. The last thing I want to do on mobile is finish typing diabe...come on, you know what I need! And then when I get there on my own, they're still suggesting solutions for challenges unrelated to me because it's part of their default nav. All this leads me to a bounce. Be assured the same is happening if your web experience is not designed to engage users. When we put out content, we need to carefully consider user experience. This means accounting for every design element, making sure your content is mobile-friendly, and creating a navigation system that's logical and intuitive.

BAD HABIT #4: PASSING THE BUCK ON EXPERIENCE

In many organizations, *experience* is one of those items that no one wants to own. In fact, it's often "Not my problem" or "I'm not given the support." A lot of this stems from a lack of designated human capital and technology to fully exploit the benefits of a better experience.

On the human capital end, much of the problem comes down to ownership. Get a marketing team together, and each will point their finger at someone else when asked who's in charge of how content is packaged. The content marketer says they are only there to create content and press publish into an existing template. The web development team says their job is just to design from templates. For either party, creating an optimal experience would require a third-party mediator.

On the tech side, the problem is compounded because most marketers still rely on their content management system (CMS) to pull together these experiences. The CMS, while very powerful, is not built for personalizing at the scale expected of modern brands. It delivers static experiences with templates, and we have to work within those confines, leaving marketers ill-equipped to do what we really need to do.

SOLUTIONS?

While I could go on and on listing out the bad habits standing in the way of a true personalized experience, the four listed here are the big ones. We'll discuss how to solve for these habits throughout the rest of the book. For now, I'll give you the short version.

First, you'll need to have an honest conversation about who owns the content experience at your organization. While there is no single answer to this question, we'll offer you some guidance in Part III. Regardless of how you approach it, the key consideration is that *someone* feels responsible for the experience in a way that stretches beyond just the quality of the content.

Second, you'll need to determine whether your CMS is equipped to deliver personalized, intuitive experiences at scale. If not, it may be time to invest in a content experience platform. You should be able to find the right combination of platform and point solutions that can help deliver better content experiences with a more targeted approach that accounts for every stage of the buyer journey.

In the not too distant future, complementing, if not altogether moving away from, a CMS is all but inevitable. As Henry Ford said, "If I had asked my customers what they wanted, they would have asked for faster horses." In other words, we can improve the capabilities of our CMS, but we can only innovate so far before we've reached its limits. Eventually we'll need to adapt to something better suited to our audience's expectation of personalized content.

To achieve results with such an increased demand for sophistication, we need to be more like Google and less like my healthcare provider. When we deliver that first piece of content to our customers, it should be the most relevant piece of content they could possibly see. There should be no guesswork, no need to weed out the crap, no excuse for your audience to leave and look for answers somewhere else.

So how do we pull that off? As we'll learn in the next chapter, it's all about the content experience.

CHAPTER 3

FOCUS ON CONTENT EXPERIENCE

___

I like beer. I'm not a beer connoisseur or anything like that, but a beer at the right time is amazing. Beer also makes for a great analogy for how I want you to think of the content experience. (Don't worry, if you're not a beer drinker, you can still enjoy this chapter. Anytime I say "beer" or "Corona," just sub in your drink of choice—a piña colada, a Manhattan, or even a Caesar if you're a fellow Canadian.)

Imagine that you're down in the basement. You know the type: one of those dark, unfinished spaces that no one in your family spends any time in unless they have to. There's a stinky wet smell down there, and the walls almost look like they are sweating for the wrong reasons.

Today, however, you have to head down to grab your tools to fix something. While you're down there, you remember the little mini fridge in the corner. "You know what?" you say to yourself. "I'm just going to grab a beer." So you do. You open the fridge, you grab a Corona, you crack the top, and you start drinking it.

Tastes pretty good, right? Of course. It's beer.

Now, I want you to imagine something a little different. Imagine you're not in the basement, but rather on a beach in Costa Rica. It's a hot day, the waves are crashing in, and the right type of sweat is happening now. Beside you is that same Corona. Everything about it is the same—the bottle, the contents, the beer temperature.

As you take a sip in paradise, for some reason, it tastes better now. It goes down smoother. The Corona tastes crisp and more refreshing than ever. All in all, this has got to be the best damn Corona you've ever had. In fact, as you look at the bottle with its little beads of condensation sliding down the side, you start thinking about how much you'd love another one.[6] Okay, now I'm going to let you stay on the beach in your mind if you want, but I want to take this analogy back to marketing. Think of that Corona as a piece of content. No matter what, it's

---

6   I'm predicting this analogy is going to lead to a huge spike in Corona sales. I'm available for sponsorships, Corona. Give me a call.

the same piece of content every time—same bottle, same label, same temperature, etc. However, the performance of that Corona (think content) depends significantly on its environment. We don't enjoy a Corona in a cold, spidery basement the same way we enjoy a Corona on a warm, inviting beach in Costa Rica.

With me so far? Great, here's the kicker: if Corona is the content, then your environment—for better or worse—is an essential piece of the content experience.

The Corona is always going to be the same. Your job is to maximize people's enjoyment of that Corona. In other words, you want to create as ideal a content experience as possible. To do that, it's not just about creating a really good collection of assets. That's the content marketers' job (and they're very good at it). Instead, it's about focusing on the environment surrounding those assets so that they work in harmony to create a memorable experience.

This distinction is important. If this book were about content marketing, then I would be spending the next several chapters telling you how to make the best beer— the ingredients, the type of barrel, the best fermentation period, etc. But again, this book isn't made for content marketers, and it's not about how to create great content. This book is for the entire marketing department and beyond, from the CMO to the demand generation marketer, even your sales leader and CEO, so that they can learn how to take great content and make it *memorable*.

For the rest of this chapter, we're going to define the essential elements of a good content experience, dispel some common misconceptions, and discuss how the content experience can be leveraged at every stage of the buyer's journey.

DEFINING THE CONTENT EXPERIENCE

A basic definition of content experience is the environment in which your content lives, how it's structured, and how it compels your prospects and customers to engage with your company. Marketers produce content in order to generate and influence leads and revenue. In order to do that successfully, we must carefully consider the environment in which our content lives.

Again, back to our Corona analogy, the content experience is the environment that surrounds us when we drink that beer. It could be a cold basement, or it could be a sunny beach. Whatever the case, that experience matters. Like it or not, we *do* judge people by the way they dress, books by their covers, wine by the label. We do the same with content. If you're trying to determine whether your content is wrapped in a good environment, you may ask yourself the following questions:

- Is it beautiful?
- Does it look professional?
- Does it capture my attention?
- Is the presentation layout engaging?
- Is it consistent with what I'd expect from my company or brand?
- Would somebody viewing this content trust our company?

Here, it's important to note that nailing one of these factors alone isn't enough to create a good content experience. In other words, building something beautiful isn't enough if the experience we create in the process is foreign to the brand. We have to tie every element together in order to build long-term trust with our company.

Appearance, design, and visual aesthetics all affect experience. It's the difference between reading an article on a Google Doc and reading it on a beautifully designed blog with images, graphics, bullet points, and subheads that all complement each other for easy reading. Look and feel intersect with user experience, but it's also much more than that.

If you've spent a lot of time and effort getting eyeballs and visitors on a particular piece of content, make sure the experience doesn't let you down. In general, 38 percent of people stop engaging with a website if the content or layout is unattractive.[7] Furthermore, the first ten seconds of the page visit are critical for users' decisions to stay or leave.[8]

WHY THE EXPERIENCE MATTERS

As you're now a good way into the book, you can tell I'm a storyteller. Don't worry, more stories to come as we go, but stick with me for the next few pages as I hit you with some hard numbers and realities that go beyond my own research and observations.

A good content experience is no different from a good customer service experience. Seventy-five percent of business buyers conduct half their research online before making an offline purchase. They are also 57 percent of the way through a purchase decision process before they engage with supply or sales reps.[9] You could also argue that as much as this book is not about content marketing, the experience matters for all the same reasons that you invested in the content in the first place.

7   Adobe, *The State of Content: Expectations on the Rise*, 2015. https://blogs.adobe.com/creative/files/2015/12/Adobe-State-of-Content-Report.pdf.

8   Chao Liu, Ryen W. White, and Susan Dumais, "Understanding Web Browsing Behaviors through Weibull Analysis of Dwell Time," *Proceedings of the 33rd International ACM SIGIR Conference on Research and Development in Information Retrieval*, 2010, 379-386.

9   Lori Wizdo. "Myth Busting 101: Insights into the B2B Buyer Journey." *Forrester*. May 25, 2015. https://go.forrester.com/blogs/15-05-25-myth_busting_101_insights_intothe_b2b_buyer_journey/.

I'm not saying that content marketing is failing you, but if it is, it may be because you're ignoring the content experience. You can have customer service reps in your organization, but if you don't have a good process and mantra for them to rally around, then you'll ultimately have bad customer service.

Like with customer service, what matters is that people brag or boo about their content experience. A positive experience bonds you to your prospective customer and helps you build trust and loyalty in your company. A negative experience can have the opposite effect, with 65 percent of buyers coming away from the buyer journey frustrated by inconsistent experiences.[10] It causes the customer to look elsewhere.

Building good vibes, trust, and optimizing content to make it look pretty and organized ultimately results in better-engaged prospects and higher conversion rates. In a recent study from Forrester, a well-designed online experience was reported to yield conversion rates 400 percent greater than online experiences that did not consider UX in their design.[11]

---

10   Oskar Lingqvist. "Do You Really Understand How Your Business Customers Buy?" *McKinsey & Company*. February 2015. https://www.mckinsey.com/business-functions/ marketing-and-sales/our-insights/do-you-really-understand-how-your-business-customers-buy

11   Laura Ramos. "Not Yet the New Normal: ABM Must Evolve into Account-Based Engagement." *Forrester*, 2018, https://www.forrester.com/report/Not+Yet+The+New+Normal+ABM+Must+E volve+Into+AccountBased+Engagement/-/E-RES118049

Furthermore, a study in *Harvard Business Review* stated that prospects who perceived content to be tailored to their specific needs were 40 percent more willing to buy from that supplier than those who didn't.[12] Personalization doesn't just mean tailoring content to a customer's interests, roles, or industries, but to specific stages of the buyer journey. This way, your buyer experiences content at the top of your funnel, converts to a marketing qualified lead (MQL) at the middle, and ultimately leads to a purchase at the bottom of the funnel. The stakes are just too high to ignore your content experience.

DIAGNOSING YOUR CONTENT EXPERIENCE

It doesn't matter whether you're still hosting your content on GeoCities (Yahoo it if you don't know it) or whether you have the most advanced site out there—everybody has a content experience. The question is whether yours is any good, or whether it's winning or losing your business. Here are some things to look out for.

PUT YOURSELF IN YOUR PROSPECTS' SHOES

Think about a common pain point that your prospects have. Type it into Google. Fingers crossed your content comes up as one of the top search results. Click into an

---

12   Karl Schmidt, Brent Adamson, and Anna Bird. "Make the Consensus Sale." *Harvard Business Review, 2015,* https://hbr.org/2015/03/making-the-consensus-sale

article and start reading. When you're finished, ask yourself the following questions:

- Did you find what you were looking for easily?
- Was it presented well and neatly laid out?
- Was it generic, or did you feel like it was speaking directly to you?
- Were you guided to another article you found useful?
- Were there too many ads, pop-ups, and distractions?
- Was the article optimized for the device you were on?

Depending on your answers, it shouldn't be too hard to determine whether the site you visited delivered a good content experience, a bad one, or merely a so-so one. Whatever you experience, good or bad, is a content experience. When you visited that site, for just a moment, you walked in the shoes of your prospect or customer. You've taken a closer look at the experience. How people consume your content and how they experience it is just as important as the words on the page.

ORGANIZATION AND STRUCTURE

When we talk about structure, we're really talking about how your content is put together—that is, how we organize content relative to other assets so that your visitors can find what they need when they come to your site or navigate to that next piece when ready for more (think

Netflix). To get a sense of your own content experience, visit your site and ask yourself the following questions:

- Can visitors navigate your site, blog, or resource library?
- Is content organized in a way that suits your prospects' needs (i.e., by topic, persona, or type)?
- Is your content in more than one place, or do people have to go searching for it?
- Can you or members of your internal team find what they're looking for?

If you've answered *no* to one or more of these questions, then it's time to reconsider the experience you're creating for your visitors and perhaps your own team. Organization, navigation, and curation affect your prospects' ability to discover useful, relevant content. If you're not making the experience easy for them, they'll simply go somewhere else. Organizing and curating content into a different and unique experience will ensure greater discoverability of your content—leading to a better content experience and an increased likelihood your visitors will share your content with others.

A GOOD CONTENT EXPERIENCE COMPELS ENGAGEMENT

When it comes to how you organize your content, you have plenty of options. However, as we discussed in the last chapter, it's probably best not to organize by content type (i.e., videos, infographics, and white papers). Remember, your prospects are far more likely to search by topic or challenge than by content type.

When we explored Spotify, we saw that structure is essential. The ability to organize content by mood, figure out who I am as an individual listener, and queue up a playlist that's tailor-made for me makes the Spotify experience special. Ultimately, that's what all of us should be thinking about when we structure our content—making the experience special. A good content experience will compel your current and prospective customers to engage and act. Our decision on whether or not to prioritize this can either compel engagement or lead to a dead end.

Not to discredit you—I know you, like every marketer, want to drive engagement. But many of us are leading audiences to dead-ends without realizing it. If we acknowledge these missteps, we can get focused on doing it right. Again, take a tip from Spotify. With every opportunity, work to make relevant personalized recommendations and include calls-to-action (CTAs) that are tailored to your buyers' interests. Consistency leads to greater trust, which compels engagement over time.

Far too often, we fail to think about the end goal when it comes to content. We're overly obsessed with engagement in one piece. We pat ourselves on the back when we get someone to engage with the content, when really the goal is to get the person to the next piece of content, and ultimately convert them on a CTA, or perhaps close the deal with attribution to the various assets involved. Take Amazon: Their goal isn't necessarily to get us to buy the one thing we need in the moment. They are trying to guide us on a path of purchases that we actually may not realize. As soon as we've selected one item, they suggest other items that are similar or other people bought as well. They've nailed the engagement piece through a strong structure and a great environment.

EVERYONE HAS A CONTENT EXPERIENCE

A content experience isn't something that you can lack. The fact of the matter is if you're producing content, there's going to be a content experience. This book is a content experience. That email you're about to look at once you've finished this chapter is another content experience—and the CTA you click on inside that email is yet another. You probably don't realize how many content experiences you're having all the time. Each one of these encounters adds up to how we feel about a company—and done right, they build the trust necessary for establishing meaningful relationships.

Knowing that, marketers have to be mindful of the kinds

of experiences we design for our customers. Going back to our Corona example, depending on the experience I design, I could encourage someone to down a whole six-pack in their basement in one sitting, or I could encourage them to relax and enjoy each sip while they soak up the sun's rays by the ocean.

In other words, how you present your content is the difference between making someone feel stressed and overloaded versus relaxed and cared for. To create an effective content experience, we must always be mindful of presenting our content at the appropriate pace, in the appropriate time, and at the appropriate place. *That's* how you get your prospects to love your brand.

When we begin to think of all our assets in this way, then we can begin to map the content experience to the buyer's journey. In the next chapter, we'll be doing exactly that, exploring some essential challenges in the most common go-to-market strategies when it comes to a complex purchase, and then discussing how a content experience can help alleviate them.

CHAPTER 4

DRIVEN BY CONTENT

Whenever we go to market, we often think our agenda is everyone else's agenda. My team and I talk about content experience all day long, so even when I'm attending conferences, I expect that all those impromptu discussions between marketers in hallways or over drinks must be focused on content experience. When I'm presenting, same thing: I'll look out into the room and picture little speech bubbles above everybody's heads, each with the words "content experience" written neatly inside them.

Sure, maybe there are a few speech bubbles here and there where people *are actually* talking about content experience, but if I'm being honest, that usually only happens when I'm forcing the conversation. For the most part, people aren't talking about content experience—not yet, anyway, and not the way they should be.

The truth is that most marketers don't think purely in terms of content experience as a strategy. Instead, we tend to talk more about how we go to market. This makes sense. We marketers have every reason to obsess over how we go to market, how we get in front of our audience, and how we capture their attention.

In a conversation with Laura Ramos, a senior analyst for Forrester, I was trying to figure out whether I should try to establish content experience as a way for brands to go to market. The other option, to me, was to concede and let the go-to-market conversation continue to be dominated by four common approaches: inbound marketing, demand generation, account-based marketing (ABM), and sales enablement.

"You know what, Randy?" Laura said. "As much as you say that they don't go to market with content experience, you look at any of these four, and it's impossible to deny how hard it is to execute on any of those strategies and go to market without delivering a piece of content."

CONTENT AT THE CORE OF CAMPAIGNS

No matter your go-to-market strategy, even if you don't think you prioritize content, you can't execute the way you want without accepting that content lies at the core of that strategy. I'll explore the four strategies mentioned above: inbound, demand generation, ABM, and sales enablement—after all, they're all driven by content.

A quick side note on the four go-to-market strategies we've selected for this book. Over time, marketing strategies come and go. A decade before this book was written, a big go-to-market strategy was social media. These days, while social media remains a big part of how brands execute their go-to-market, it is not a go-to-market strategy in and of itself. The four strategies discussed here are central to how we do business, and for a lot of other companies as well. If you have a different set of core go-to-market strategies, or if three years down the road there's a whole new set of approaches that work better than the ones listed here, then feel free to sub those in. Ultimately, the point is that regardless of your go-to-market approach, it will involve leveraging content to reach your audience one way or another.

When you look at it this way, it's no surprise that brands are creating more content than ever. Every year, in survey after survey, somewhere around 70 percent of marketers indicate their plans to produce more content than they had the previous year. As more companies go all-in, the amount of content available to us as consumers is staggering. That's okay if that content is there to support other strategies. However, that's not often the case. As we discussed, too often, the content we create is never used.

If we truly want to be successful in how we leverage our content as we go to market, we have to keep the content experience front and center, connecting our content to the buyer journey in a way that is useful to the consumer. This concept is hit on by my friend Robert Rose and his co-author Carla Johnson in their book *Experiences: The 7th Era of Marketing*. In chapter 4, they hit on a similar idea of "'content-driven experiences'" to enable and empower connections through experiences. They enforce that your role as a marketer is to deeply understand your buyers, since they are now in control of their own journey, and create experiences so mesmerizing and valuable that they *want* to take that next step.

As I walk you through these four go-to-market strategies, consider the different stages of the buyer journey—awareness, engagement, consideration, decision, and advocacy. The goal of this chapter is to be able to think through any go-to-market strategy and explore how a better focus on content experience can improve your chances for success. Think about the experiences you need to create beyond simply what you sell that will resonate with your audience and provide deep value to their role (and lives).

INBOUND

HubSpot deserves a lot of credit for popularizing the term and concept of inbound marketing, for good or bad.

Essentially, it goes something like this: if we put content out there that is relevant and helpful, then people will start to trust us as we interact with them using various methods of communication.

My good friend and respected marketing thought leader Marcus Sheridan likes to tell the story of running a pool company during the recession of 2008. The economic downturn hit them pretty hard, as it had with most businesses, but Sheridan and his team were able to figure out a simple, creative save for the business. Using their blog, they became a trusted resource for questions about pools, answering common searches like, "What is a fiberglass inground pool?" By answering these questions well, Google indexed them at the top of their search results, which led to a huge influx of interest in their business.

Content is a huge part of inbound. Marketers like Sheridan understood that being discovered through search was only the beginning. If, after clicking, the customer discovered that they weren't being offered anything of value, they would simply click away and head to the next search result. If, however, the content *was* valuable and customers did stick around to read it, marketers faced a new challenge: keeping them immersed so the next piece of content aligns with the thing that first caught their eye.

In Sheridan's world, if the first piece of content was about the benefits of fiberglass pools, the next piece should be about something related, like caring for pools in the winter. Chronological order, he reasoned, wasn't good enough. What if the next post was about something completely unrelated, like an article on hot tubs?

Effective inbound marketing, then, is about giving someone a ride to the next content asset and recommending something that seemed like a good contextual fit. Make the experience better, and it will be easier to convert someone into a lead when they're ready to learn more.

One B2B company that has mastered the art of inbound marketing is Pivotal, a software company that unleashes developer productivity and transforms how the world builds software. When Pivotal brings people in to a piece of content, they don't simply drop them into a stream of all their latest blog posts or presentations. If they're targeting a CIO, for instance, they have a specific "stream" built out for people with that job title. This focused content stream, some of which is handpicked and some of which is AI-recommended, ensures that everything the CIO sees is relevant and continues to push them through the buyer journey. This approach ensures a focus on structure and increases the chances of engagement.

DEMAND GENERATION

Some people might argue that inbound is a subcategory of demand generation, or vice versa. Still, many marketers have different job titles based on one or the other, and regardless of whether one is a subcategory of the other, each has its nuances.

Demand generation is focused on driving awareness and interest in a company's products or services once they have shown interest—it's about getting past the lead and driving them into the pipeline. In other words, demand generation is a marriage of marketing programs with a structured sales process. Compared to inbound, demand generation is often a more integrated marketing strategy that is deployed after the lead has been captured.

To give you an idea of how important demand generation has become, at Uberflip, our content team works closely with the demand generation team to understand what specific content is needed to fuel our campaigns.

The days of high-fiving everyone after getting a lot of eyeballs to a single content asset or earning a whole bunch of clicks to a link in an email are gone. As marketers, our job is to drive people to revenue. That's the ultimate goal of demand generation—building trust by continuing to drive your target buyers through the funnel, with content as a driving force. After all, according to IDG, people are far more likely to make a purchase decision after they've seen at least seven pieces of content. The question is, how do we deliver a content experience that propels prospects to self-nurture?

One company that's done an excellent job of answering this question is Blackbaud. Once they have identified contacts to nurture, they don't just send out emails with the hope of getting a click. They build personalized content experiences that not only have beautiful and consistent designs that flow from emails to stream to individual content assets, but they structure it in a way that once someone clicks on that CTA, they're dropped into a content stream that's specific to the industry and stage of the journey. By delivering a better, more personalized, and binge-worthy experience, Blackbaud is able to build trust with their target buyer and help that person understand how their service can solve the customer's needs.

ACCOUNT-BASED MARKETING (ABM)

ABM has caught marketers' attention by storm—look no further than its ascent on Gartner's Hype Cycle. ABM involves identifying accounts that we believe we can land and then developing a targeted approach to landing those accounts. Jon Miller (our Foreword author) put it best: rather than fishing with a net, it's about fishing with a spear. We get exactly what we're hunting for by using a precision-based approach.

At any rate, the fundamental question driving ABM is how to best cater to the accounts we want to land. In the early days of ABM, marketers put most of their focus on selecting desirable accounts and then organizing them in *tiers* (Google Jon Miller/Engagio's *Clear and Complete Guide to ABM* if you need a 101 here). Little thought went into how to actually engage them—this is where content plays a key role. Today, ABM is far more relationship-focused, with marketers deploying a whole array of strategies to draw their target buyers in with personalized content at the core of their ABM strategy.

For instance, one popular ABM approach is to send direct mail to the account, perhaps in the form of a thoughtful gift. After the marketing team has grabbed the account's attention, however, the question becomes how to continue to deliver information that feels personalized. Even if we could afford to send more gifts, it loses its novelty. A company called Snowflake excels at what comes next and how they incorporate content. As part of the data warehousing business, Snowflake operates in a highly competitive, and completely unsexy, environment. However, the experiences Snowflake is able to drop their accounts into at every step of the journey are very sexy—in marketing terms, that is. For instance, if Snowflake were trying to land Pepsi as a customer, they'd start with ads that show Pepsi and Snowflake working closely together. Then, instead of sending the people at Pepsi to some generic link to a page that talks up their business, they'd send them to a personalized content destination designed for this specific customer. We'll dig deeper on the example of how Snowflake does this right in the next part of this book.

SALES ENABLEMENT

Gone are the days where we say marketing deals with marketing problems and sales deals with sales problems. We use terms like *smarketing* to acknowledge that the two are fundamentally interrelated. Modern marketing extends beyond the marketing-qualified lead (MQL) to concepts like opportunity creation and advocacy. If you live outside of the B2B world, just think of the path of your buyer from top to bottom of funnel.

As marketers, when we create an email drip campaign in our marketing automation platform, we obsess over every email, the words that go into them, the links, and everything beyond. Yet we look away and ignore these obsessions over details when it comes to the communication coming from our sales teams.

As a CMO, I get too many emails where someone is

trying to sell me everything under the sun. The copy has so many links that it looks like a bad bruise—with black-and-blue text littered all over an email. I've coined this "the black and blue email." I don't know about you, but when I'm staring down six to twelve (or more) hyperlinks, I have no idea where I'm supposed to click first.

Even if I do click on a link, I have no idea where I'm supposed to go next. Should I wander around their website, or should I head back to the email to figure out which link I should click next? Meanwhile, while I'm wasting my time swimming around in this black-and-blue ocean, forty other emails have popped into my inbox with the exact same kind of overwrought message, and I'm no better off for any of it. To say the least, that's not an especially good content experience.

Not all sales enablement is so sloppy. One company that does an especially good job is Terminus (ironically an account-based marketing platform). When their sales reps engage with a contact or an account (or what they call a "future customer") they're trying to land, the marketing team sets up that rep so they can hand-pick the right pieces of content personalized to the prospect. The Terminus team drops future customers into a one-to-one experience that contains content relevant to their role and includes a personalized video to humanize the connection with their brand. This approach demonstrates a commitment to structure and relevance, which is central to the content experience. The ability to be nimble aligns well to research from Gartner (CEB), showing that 6.8 different individuals will weigh in to the B2B buying decision.[13] Their sales reps can easily spin up one-to-one experiences for each member of the buying committee.

BEYOND THE DEAL

I know I said I'd focus on four common approaches, but don't overlook how key a focus on content experience can be at every stage from every department. Content is key to engaging our new, renewing, or at-risk customers. The experience ensures that those customers follow a journey and can speak as an extension of your mission. Although we won't dive into examples here, give consideration to the way you leverage content to onboard, train, and tell stories about your best customers.

MOVING ON

As you reflect back on the examples outlined, you can easily check off the focus on the environment, structure, and engagement—and, in turn, content experience. Now that we've touched on the four approaches, it's fair to say that whether we realize it or not, we're driving people to content with a content experience at every step. You can

---

13   Challenger Sales, 2018, https://www.challengerinc.com/sales/.

no longer say you don't have a content experience. The question to reflect on is what we began with: do you have a good content experience or a bad one at every stage of your journey?

PART II

HOW TO PERSONALIZE CONTENT EXPERIENCES AT SCALE

Since you've made it this far, you must agree that no matter your go-to-market strategy, executing it requires not only great content, but also a great content experience to match. With so many different strategies, and so many different buyers to appeal to, your entire team needs to be aligned around the content experience. It's the only way to deliver on expectations consistently day in and day out.

In Part II, we'll answer the question that I just know is on the tip of your tongue: "Now that I've bought into the content experience, how the f#ck am I going to do this every day, multiple times a day, across a global organization?" Where Part I was all about the *why* of the content experience, Part II is about the *how*.

CHAPTER 5

EMBRACE FRAMEWORKS

———

Don't fret. Don't fear. This chapter is not going to be where your reading experience turns into a textbook. Yes, this chapter will introduce you to the Content Experience Framework, and I know our eyes tend to glaze over with each new framework we see, but come on, frameworks aren't all bad.

Seriously, I mean it. In this mercifully short chapter, I'll explain why.

A FEW CLASSIC FRAMEWORKS

Over the years, a lot of great frameworks have helped us think more methodically about our marketing process. Let's see if my top three frameworks match up with yours.

PEOPLE, PROCESS, AND TECHNOLOGY

One of my favorite, more general frameworks is the idea of people, process, and technology. As a CMO, I hate it when people rush to buy up a whole bunch of technology and say, "If we buy a whole bunch of technology and hire a bunch of people, that will solve the problem." This simple framework reminds us that's not true. We have to start by looking at the right people and processes *before* making any sort of tech purchase.

In the last part of the book, we spoke about a company called Snowflake. Daniel Day, Director of ABM and Market Planning, is a great example of this. When he wanted to build more engaging content experiences for targeted accounts, he didn't start with a ton of tech. He built a rock star team as his first step and hacked away at a template to produce about a dozen of his ideal content destinations filled with handpicked targeted content. Then the magic happened; he started to see great engagement, and his execs saw it, too. They called him in to a meeting and said, "We're not sure how you're creating all the engagement, but we want more." That's when he realized that he had the right framework but couldn't scale until he added the right technology. That's why, to me, technology is often the last but most important piece to achieve scale.

THE UNIVERSITY CLASSICS

In the natural process of my coursework while completing my undergrad and MBA degrees, I found myself listing *the four Ps*—product, price, promotion, and placement (maybe there's a fifth these days, I can't keep track)—all the time. And let's not forget our friend the SWOT analysis, which could help me determine whether a strategy was silly or sound. I'm sure you learned similar, if not the same, classic frameworks during your college days, too. And although I didn't have the opportunity to learn the stages of the sales funnel in school, I'm sure many people reading this book would have seen it creep into textbooks or PowerPoints in the last decade or so (unless they are still teaching selling widgets via Acme Co.).

MODERN FRAMEWORKS

These days, plenty of other frameworks have helped us inform the strategies that ultimately led to our Content Experience Framework. For instance, we owe a great deal to HubSpot for teaching us to appreciate the value of inbound and introducing the HubSpot Inbound Methodology. This methodology taught us that relevant and helpful content can attract, convert, and close leads for your business. Another more recent framework that I love is FlipMyFunnel, with credit to my friend Sangram at Terminus, which has helped me understand how to effectively leverage the account-based methodology.

INTRODUCING THE CONTENT EXPERIENCE FRAMEWORK

The best frameworks help us understand a new concept in a way that is both memorable and simple, very much like what the examples above have done for us. That's my goal with the Content Experience Framework that I'm about to introduce and explore over the next several chapters.

The Content Experience Framework is focused on how to personalize content experiences at scale. For clarity's sake, that does not and will not include how to create better content or how to be more efficient with which content assets are created. That would be more of a content marketing framework—and as we repeated throughout Part I, that's simply not what this book is about. If you're looking for a content marketing framework, you'll have plenty out there to choose from.

I'll admit that years ago, even my Uberflip co-founder, Yoav Schwartz, and I tried to suggest a content marketing framework before I waved the white flag and conceded the term to content creation. The concept was based on four pillars that looked at Creation, *Experience*, Distribution, and Insights. We had great engagement and views come from our community through developing a tech stack builder (which Yoav really championed) that helped marketers see what tools/platforms helped with different stages. It's still alive out there if you want to take grademystack.com for a ride.

But as time passed, it was obvious content experience was bigger than a pillar of content marketing, although my aforementioned friend Robert Rose and I have had fun debates on the topic over the years. But here we are, Content Experience is real. Not just because of this book, but even G2 Crowd (a peer-to-peer technology review platform) recognizes content experience with a distinct grid for how people are solving for their tech stack.

And so, we are ready for a framework. The Content Experience Framework centers around a simple idea: Now that you've got all this great content, how do you use it in a way that fosters more genuine, personalized connections with your audience?

The Content Experience Framework isn't something I whipped up over a few Coronas in my basement. This framework has come out of the countless conversations I've had with marketers just like you, who have shared their best practices for avoiding the kinds of pitfalls we discussed in the earlier chapters.

As we work through each stage in the following chapters, some of you may feel more confident in how you're achieving one stage over another. That's okay. This framework is designed to unite multiple people from your organization to GSD (get sh#t done). If you're a VP or CMO, this is your opportunity to ensure that you've got ownership over the different stages to show people what could happen with better collaboration.

So, without further ado, I present to you the Content Experience Framework.

Content Experience Framework

The Best Way to Create Personalized Content Experiences

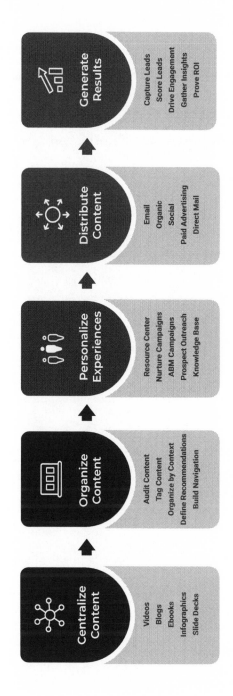

Centralize Content
- Videos
- Blogs
- Ebooks
- Infographics
- Slide Decks

Organize Content
- Audit Content
- Tag Content
- Organize by Context
- Define Recommendations
- Build Navigation

Personalize Experiences
- Resource Center
- Nurture Campaigns
- ABM Campaigns
- Prospect Outreach
- Knowledge Base

Distribute Content
- Email
- Organic
- Social
- Paid Advertising
- Direct Mail

Generate Results
- Capture Leads
- Score Leads
- Drive Engagement
- Gather Insights
- Prove ROI

Presented By überflip

Over the next five chapters, you will begin to understand how this framework applies to what you're doing and how other marketers are executing in their organization. I assure you, this will not feel like your year-two university textbook on how to handle a marketing project.

Before we dive in, one last note on technology. This framework is designed to help you put some fundamental practices in place so you can scale your content experience efforts to fit your organizational needs. While a dedicated content experience platform will help you execute, you can also get results by deploying whatever set of tools, spreadsheets, and serious hacking skills you have available to you. The concepts remain the same either way.

CHAPTER 6

CENTRALIZE

———

I can't tell you how many people I run into saying things like, "I don't have enough content to even begin to create a content experience, let alone power all my go-to-market strategies!"

I call BS.

But it continues to happen. Literally while I was editing this book, someone reached out for advice saying, "My team wants to focus on the experience, but I don't think we have enough content."

As I alluded to in the introduction, modern marketers are hardwired to stress out daily over whether they're creating enough content to fulfill their audience's thirst for knowledge and insights. They almost certainly are. Most marketers shouldn't be worrying about whether they're creating enough content, but what they're going to do with all the content they've already created over the past few days, weeks, months, and even years.

You're maybe tired of the previous stat I gave on content usage, but good (or bad) news, I found another tied to our sales teams that shows only one in five assets created by marketing for sales teams is used.[14] This is a company-wide problem! Most organizations have plenty of great content. Sure, some of it may become dated, but hopefully most of it is evergreen (or can be updated). With a content audit, I am sure you'll find a lot of that content would align perfectly to campaigns throughout the buyer's journey. Too often, however, the reality is that once it's produced, this great content is left to twist in the wind—unused and forgotten, but still a valuable asset in its own right.

One of my good friends, the Queen of Content, if you will, Ann Handley, refers to these pieces as *homeless content*. No doubt, your organization has plenty of its own homeless content—the decks your team uploaded to SlideShare, the videos you posted to YouTube, and all those sad and lonely infographics on our blogs. As Ann likes to say, it's

---

14 Robert Rose, *Content Marketing: Unlocking Sales & Marketing Performance,* Content Marketing Institute and LinkedIn, 2018, https://business.linkedin.com/content/dam/me/business/en-us/marketing-solutions/resources/pdfs/cmi-linkedin-research.pdf.

time for that content to come home and get comfortable, to kick off its shoes and relax on the sofa.

That's precisely the goal of our first phase in the Content Experience Framework. So get ready, it's time to put up some twinkle lights, cue up our favorite Spotify playlist, and welcome our favorite pieces of content back home.

REMEMBER THAT DEWEY DECIMAL SYSTEM

Indexing your content may not be the sexiest concept (yet those sexy librarians could always find everything amid thousands of books), but it's the foundation of building a world-class content experience and the chapters to follow. Here, the benefits to your organization should be obvious:

- Indexing helps you understand and track all of your content assets.
- Indexing helps you make more informed decisions on what content you're going to leverage.
- Indexing reduces the likelihood that you'll duplicate your efforts and produce a piece of content that already exists.

While a dedicated software platform can always help,

basic indexing can be accomplished with something as simple as a spreadsheet. (Microsoft Excel will never die!) Simply list out your assets in the first column and then use the other columns to fill in the relevant details—such as format, topic, headline, CTA, persona, keyword, journey stage, and so on.

This is the most basic version of indexing that you can safely get away with. It's easily searchable, can quickly tell you where a particular asset lives, and requires very little budget to set up and maintain. And with modern day team collaboration tools, this can be an online internal resource that everyone on your team can access.

That said, it does require some time, and at some point, you'll have more assets than your spreadsheet can handle. Switching to a database or dedicated content experience platform (CEP) at this point will help you better integrate content into your feed, no matter whether the asset is a blog post, a deck on SlideShare, or a video on YouTube. Tools like a CEP help you integrate all of your marketing content into one central location so that you can easily take stock of the content you have and where it can be used.

WHY CENTRALIZATION MATTERS

I've always found it interesting that many of the definitions of content marketing refer to *owned* content. But in many cases, we end up housing that content on sites we don't own at all! YouTube, LinkedIn, Twitter—these are owned by Google, Microsoft, and who knows where Twitter will land one day. I'm not suggesting we shouldn't *lend* our content to these places for people to discover. Sharing your content to these external channels is a great way to get eyes on your content and hook and capture your audience. But a lot of our discussions through this book have been about guiding someone through a journey.

With every piece of content, you should be thinking about how you can bring the experience inbound so that you can serve up the next great asset to your audience without losing prospects to the infinite scroll of other outbound channels. When you index and centralize your content, you take the first step toward creating your own infinite scroll.

We all know that experience when we're on YouTube and we watch a video about, say, digital cameras, perhaps a kickass Sony camera. As soon as we're done with that Sony video, YouTube recommends a Nikon camera video, or worse, a video of a cat that can take pictures—weird but true. We do this in more ways than we care to admit. How often do you link someone in a tweet to a video you produced on YouTube? I know we want to increase our followers on these channels, but wouldn't you rather increase your revenue? When we welcome home our content, we're able to take control of these journeys.

Now, there are ways to do this better. Ending every video with a strong call-to-action, for instance, could certainly help pull your audience toward more of your owned properties. A far easier way is to stop relying on outbound channels to deliver information. Get them inbound with that first tweet. Then—because you've done such a good job centralizing your content—you can follow up with a pitch-perfect package of content that helps personalize the experience and keep your audience moving through the buyer's journey.

A bright marketer I know named Stephanie Totty, whose career took off at a company called ExamSoft, recently started taking a proactive approach to indexing her content. Once she started to do this, she quickly realized the number of assets her company had created over the past four years, and how many of those were going unused. About 15–20 percent of the content she dug up was content that they should have been using on an ongoing basis but hadn't touched in quite some time. She was sick over all the work that had gone into the creation with no actual return from a marketing or lead generation standpoint. This was when Stephanie started to map all her content to her personas, which in turn helped her extend the content's shelf life once it was in her control, indexed, and easily searchable for her and her team.

KEEP IT TOGETHER

Centralizing is the first phase toward being able to step back, take stock of everything you have, sort it, and then package it based on topic, stage of the funnel, and buyer persona—regardless of content type. As we progress toward the next steps—namely, organize and personalize—you will see how the value of centralizing becomes essential. Not only does it help you keep better track of your outbound assets, but it also helps you better understand, package, and leverage your content across various marketing approaches like the ones explored in chapter 4.

Remember, it takes multiple assets—seven or more—to get someone through the buyer journey. Instead of having to endlessly churn out more content to reach those seven touchpoints, centralizing allows you to understand all the assets at your disposal and how to put them to work.

So here's my call-to-action for this chapter: Find a way to pull that content together. Connect that content. Make sure there's a person on your team who can organize that content and own that responsibility. Once your content is centralized in one location, there's not a lot of extra work that needs to be done here. The work really starts when we get into organizing all those assets, which is step two.

CHAPTER 7

ORGANIZE

———

It's sad to now think of all the VHS tapes and DVDs out there that no longer have a home. They used to be a big deal, but now they're simply homeless content left over from the Blockbuster era (other than the last few I never returned. If Blockbuster ever comes back, I probably owe $24,000 in late fees now). Blockbuster is an interesting story because of how fast and hard they went under. Unless you're an especially young reader, I'm sure you remember what it was like to go to Blockbuster. If you were anything like me, the whole experience was pure torture—except for the part where I got to grab my favorite candy on the way out.

Let's journey way back to the far distant past of 1995, when Blockbuster was thriving! On this day, I want to watch *Apollo 13* starring Tom Hanks. Finding it is pretty easy, since it's still in the New Releases section, and I know it will be sorted alphabetically under *A*. However, say on my return to the store I'm in a Tom Hanks mood and I want to have a little marathon of his movies that night with my friends. In such a situation, I don't have many options. I can't just go up to the Blockbuster staff and say, "Hey, where's your Tom Hanks section?" It's up to me to remember what other movies star Hanks and then decide what genre they're sorted under. Is *Forrest Gump* a comedy, action, or a drama? (I know you're debating it now.) What about *Big, Turner and Hooch*, or *The Burbs*? Some answers may be easier than others, but finding everything is still going to require a good amount of guesswork.

Part of this is due to the way movies were organized in your typical Blockbuster. I remember walking in circles trying to figure out what movie to watch—and a lot of times, I left without anything, saying, "Argh, I'll just find something on TV." In terms of content experience, Blockbuster wasn't great. It's no wonder they went bankrupt.[15]

So what went wrong for Blockbuster? As I've already alluded to, a big problem was in how they organized their content. Sure, they had physical limitations to deal with, but all they really needed to improve the experience

---

15 Side note: As of this writing, there is still one Blockbuster left, and their Twitter account, @ loneblockbuster, is pretty hilarious.

was a book—or perhaps even a computer terminal—that allowed customers to search by different categories.

Fast forward to the modern era, where we all bow down to the powerhouse known as Netflix. The Netflix experience trumps Blockbuster in many ways, but a big key to their success is how good they are at organizing their content. They tag every film, TV show, and documentary with tons of different searchable criteria, including cast, genre, and director. They even know what content is similar and are so good at providing recommendations that we'll binge for hours watching program after program without having to lift a finger. Thanks to Netflix, if I'm in a Tom Hanks mood, all I have to do is search for his name, and their whole Tom Hanks library is immediately available.

I could go on, but I'm sure you've heard some version of the Blockbuster vs. Netflix story before. I use it here because it shows the two different extremes of an organized content experience. Sadly, for many brands, their organization is still more akin to Blockbuster's than it is to Netflix's. They may have tons of amazing ebooks, videos, or blog posts, but they're all organized in a single arbitrary way.

Now, I want you to think about your own organization's strategy. Is all your content grouped together by format? Can visitors find it any other way? Remember, people come to your site searching for solutions—and the more time you expect them to spend doing that, the more likely they are to look for their solutions somewhere else.

That can't happen if you're truly invested in creating a great content experience for your buyers. That's why it's our responsibility as marketers to tie our content together in meaningful, intuitive ways so that people don't have to pull their hair out trying to find it.

BEGINNING THE ORGANIZING PROCESS

As long as you've invested your time in centralizing your content (as outlined in the previous chapter), you have a huge head start on the task ahead of you. The next step, which many of us tend to skip, is taking the time to audit and tag the content you have. It's not a fun task, but it's the reason Netflix's market is now north of $150 billion.[16]

But where do we start? We have so much content—we've agreed on that much so far. Is this going to be impossible? I assure you not—even Spotify, which has over 30 million songs, takes time to organize their content. While some

---

16   Rani Molla, "Netflix Is Now Worth More Than Comcast," *Recode,* May 23, 2018, https://www. recode.net/2018/5/23/17386696/netflix-reed-hastings-comcast-worth-more.

of this is done with machine learning, some of that is still done with a human touch, as it requires human intervention to set the machines and algorithms up to produce what Spotify terms powerful "algotorial" recommendations. So it's possible. We just have to start by asking the right questions:

- What are your topics?
- Who are your personas?
- Will you organize your content by stage of the funnel?
- What kind of content do you have?

Regardless of whatever tagging and organizing choices are the right call for you, it's going to take a full content audit to complete this stage correctly. Find out what you have, tag it, and make it easy to be found in a personalized manner.

Another benefit of auditing your assets is that it will reveal gaps that you will want to fill. For example, you may find you're lacking content for the middle of your buyer journey, which may be a reason why your company often stalls out halfway through the sales cycle. Once labeled, your content can be categorized for easy discoverability on the front-end through the top navigation, and on the back-end, either through a spreadsheet or using a CEP and/or other specific MarTech. This will allow you to quickly and easily build personalized experiences at any time.

ORGANIZING = DISCOVERABILITY

Have you ever created that perfect piece of content and sent it out through your normal channels only to have no one notice it? "Why isn't anyone reading this?" you shout to no one in particular from your desk. "It's *so good.*"

Of course that's happened to you. It's happened to all of us.

Luckily, we have an answer to this most frustrating of marketing conundrums. Sure, your content may be the best thing since sliced bread, but if no one is looking at it, it probably means *no one can find it.* It's buried under a mountain of blogs, ebooks, videos, infographics, and webinars. It's been pushed to the deepest, darkest corner of your content library. Without a map, iron will, and night vision goggles, no one is going to find it.

The problem with your content is not that it isn't good; it's just not easily accessible. You, like many B2B marketers, have neglected your content discoverability. Content discoverability is the findability of your content within your blog, resource library, or other public-facing content destination. Sure, good SEO can help your content rank high on Google, but SEO is a tactic to drive website traffic. Once you've attracted traffic to your site, how easy is it for a person to move from asset to asset? Can they find all that kickass content you've produced without having to set out on an epic quest or back to a new Google search?

Discoverability is all about how you structure your content—and it's one of the key components of content experience. Here are a number of suggestions to improve your content discoverability.

ORGANIZE IT THE WAY PEOPLE ACTUALLY LOOK FOR IT

The default way of organizing content is from newest to oldest. Hell, we all do it. There's something about putting your freshest content up that makes us feel like we're on top of things. Really, this is only noticeable to that small percentage of devoted fans who come back to your site daily. To the casual drop-in, the recency of a post doesn't matter much. What does matter, however, is whether they know how to find what they're looking for when they do land on your site.

Some of the most effective ways of organizing content are by persona or job title, by topic, by industry, and by vertical. As with all things, some experimentation will help you understand what works best for your audiences. In the past, my team has organized things a bunch of different ways using heat-mapping tools like Hotjar to see what categories get the most clicks from our audience. For our purposes, we discovered that organizing by content topic was far and away the best performer.

DEVISE A NAVIGATIONAL PATH

Let's remember, our goal is to guide someone on a path to purchase. How are you going to organize your navigation to follow that? For instance, within your blog, if you're building specific streams of content, or perhaps a microsite, how have you laid it out so that your visitors are navigating to the next asset? When it comes to navigation, here are two things to keep in mind:

First, we all love Google—it's taught us to search and we will find. So let's play along. Better buyers search on your site then head back to Google—right? Search bars enable users to quickly determine whether you have anything in your library that aligns with their interests—although your content will only be searchable if you've tagged it properly (more on that in the next section).

Second, sometimes buyers know exactly what they're looking for when they visit your site, but other times it takes a word or two to jog their memory. One way to make search even easier is with headings. How many menu headings do you have across your navigation bar? Think of these headings as suggested filters for your audience. Are you taking advantage of this prime real estate? Once you've thought through the different ways to organize your content, plot them across your navigation bar with separate menu headings. When it comes to basic navigation considerations such as these, I've found that the more options we provide, the greater the likelihood that one of them will hit the nail on the head for our prospects.

TAG IT

Metadata tagging is another great way to make sure your content is discoverable for an external audience. Most likely, you already know that, and I'm not going to get all technical on you here. The question is, how should you approach the tagging process?

The short answer is that your tagging considerations are fully based on your content strategy and how you're going to market. That said, I know it's useful to have a real-world example or two, so here's a high-level look at how our team answers the tagging question at Uberflip:

◆ TAGGING STRUCTURE

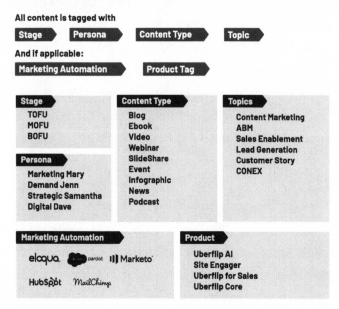

Here, you can see that we're particularly focused on a few elements for our buyers:

- Topic
- Stage of the buyer journey
- Persona
- Content type
- Marketing automation platform
- Whether the asset discusses a specific product

Tagging along these basic parameters has greatly improved our ability to find and provide the right content at the right time. For instance, one of our marketers might say, "I need a middle-of-the-funnel piece for demand generation. It needs to be X persona, and it needs to be a video." Then, they'll filter for those needs and select the piece of content that best fits those criteria.

MAXIMIZE AI

AI is a hot topic for marketers right now and will only increase in applicability post-publish date of this book. AI is progressing on a daily basis in terms of the capabilities and functionalities. To make a complex conversation simple, if you're able to tie AI to your content, it dramatically improves your ability to recommend new assets by drawing from large sets of consumption and third-party intent data. Again, when your sales depend on your ability to move people through seven, eight, nine pieces of content (or even just three if your journey is simpler), your ability to provide strong recommendations is crucial to accelerating pipeline velocity.

Having a data-backed recommendation strategy is essential to having a strong content experience. It's one of the best ways to keep your prospects moving and get them where they need to be. You can do this manually by applying insights from your analytics to set the path, but investing in an AI recommendation engine is crucial to scale. Yes, it's an up-front investment, but it'll pay for itself pretty quickly in the hours of labor it saves you.

AI will help you personalize and scale your content. Whether you can invest in it or not, you should still be trying to use the analytics and the data you have to set that recommendation path manually. Really, it's worth the investment so you can scale and offer your customers a truly personalized experience based on what they've been looking at.

DON'T WAIT UP

Now that we've had our discussion about organization, I'll leave you with a warning: *put in the work as you go.* Seriously. Especially when it comes to tagging, make these steps part of the process. It will take an additional thirty seconds—if that—to do it right. If you don't tag as you go, then good luck to you, because you've just created a lot of work for your team on the back-end once you start to scale your content efforts. The longer you wait, the more work you're creating down the road. And we're not talking hours here—more like days, weeks, or even months. Trust us. We didn't invest in tagging early enough and had to learn this lesson the hard way.

The good news was, once we learned our lesson and solved our tagging problem, our content picture came sharply into focus. It wasn't the prettiest picture we'd ever seen—90 percent of our content was focused on the top of our sales funnel—but that insight allowed us to build a much better content strategy moving forward and moved us closer to where we needed to be.

Here's the bottom line: by putting a priority on organizing, other members of your marketing and sales team can easily find and share your marketing content. You remove the need for the (sexy) librarian who's the only one who can navigate your long history of content! This becomes extremely useful when planning nurture sequences, performing sales outreach, or following up with prospective buyers. This is a little bit of a bold statement on my part, but I'm willing to bet that all of your unused content will come back into play if you don't skimp here. Besides, it will make our next step, personalize, a whole hell of a lot easier.

CHAPTER 8

PERSONALIZE

One of my best friends is named Jay. We've been friends since kindergarten, we went to the same schools all the way through high school, and we even lived together in university. These days, we have kids about the same age, and we talk all the time.

Although we share a lot of similarities, Jay and I are very different when it comes to dealing with technology, especially when it comes to willingness for tech to do what it does in the background: track us. If you ask me, track anything I do because I know it delivers a better, more personalized experience. Ask Jay, and he is genuinely worried about being tracked, as if it's some tremendous invasion of privacy.

I don't want to rip on Jay too much. After all, I get his concern. Some of it comes down to him not understanding how things work. I'll even say this to him: "I don't get your concern with tracking, Jay. I know you love Netflix. You watch it all the time at home, and so do your kids."

"No, no, no," he'll say. "Netflix is different."

"Well, how is it different? What do you like about Netflix?"

"I like that it recommends good shows for me."

"You like that they're able to make such good recommendations because they're tracking what you do, right?"

"No, no, no," he'll say again. "That's different. That's contained inside of Netflix. I trust them."

"Fair enough. What about Google? When you get on Google, perform a search, and they deliver results that are relevant to you, how do you think they do that?"

"They just deliver the most popular results," he'll say.

"Maybe that was true ten or fifteen years ago, but that's not true anymore. These days, Google's algorithm works to deliver results that are meaningful to *you*—right down to your neighborhood, the time of day, and what other people similar to you in your area are doing. I bet you use

Google a lot to make decisions on what to buy and what restaurants to go to."

"That's different, too. That's Google. They're more contained."

I get why he feels that way, but for many of us, the only real difference between Netflix, Google, and any other brand that tracks our behaviors is the degree to which we trust them. That's why, for any modern organization, trust is a big, big deal.

THE VALUE OF PERSONALIZATION

In the current era, consumers have learned to decide very quickly whether they trust your brand. If you can deliver a seamless personalized experience like Netflix and Google, then your customers are happy to open up their privacy gates and allow themselves to be tracked. If we fail to offer this kind of experience, then our customers will reflexively pull back and clamp down on the data they allow us to see.[17]

---

17   For more on this, see: Greg Sterling, "Survey: 99 Percent of Customers Will Share Personal Info for Rewards, But Want Brands to Ask Permission," *Marketing Land*, June 2, 2015, https://marketingland.com/survey-99-percent-of-consumers-will-share-personal-info-for-rewards-also-want-brands-to-ask-permission-130786.

Customers, regardless of B2C or B2B, will happily volunteer their information to get a better experience, but only if we operate in a way that shows we can be trusted with it and that we won't use it inappropriately. To build that trust, we have to show that we can add value and be relatable at the end of the day—just like our friends at Netflix and Google. In chapter 1, we referenced those moments when we decide whether to let an app track our location and data. Those decisions are instantaneous, but they are based on the same association Jay has to trust. I assure you that in the modern day, post-GDPR marketing world, as we request consent to track activity, your audience is making the same split-second decision. Do I trust these guys? The key to doing so is showing out of the gate that we can and will continue to deliver a meaningful and personalized content experience. The question for the B2B marketer is, how do we create these at scale?

To answer that question, we're going to spend most of this chapter examining the four marketing strategies we first laid out in chapter 4: inbound, demand generation, ABM, and sales enablement. But before we do that, let's all make sure we agree on what personalization means to the modern marketer.

PERSONALIZATION CAN BE OVERWHELMING

If all you had to do to personalize was make it so your

website greeted every visitor by name ("Welcome, Randy!"), then we wouldn't have much to talk about in this chapter. We'd just tell you to buy a solution like Optimizely, and you'd be off to the races. Same thing when your latest email could start with "Hey Randy" and we were amazed at how they knew! Today, we quickly chalk that up to basic marketing automation if the rest of the email doesn't match our wants/needs.

Our buyers expect more. The people coming to your site looking for solutions are on a complicated journey. It's going to take more than a robot that can learn their name to impress them. Remember, it takes a lot of content to convert a visitor into a qualified lead. To make sure you're getting the right content in front of them, you'll need to use every tactic you have available—such as lead nurturing, sales coordination, and targeted account mapping—all while demonstrating your credibility and trustworthiness.

To show you what I mean, let's take a look at two personalization experiences I had recently.

Sometimes, my dad likes to help as Uberflip's sales rep. When he learned that one of his friends' companies was looking to improve their digital marketing, he suggested they contact us to see if we'd be a good fit for them.

Wanting to learn more about the company, I headed over

to their website and started clicking around. On their content page where they kept their white papers, I saw something odd. Underneath a little teaser for the company's most recent white paper, their call-to-action simply read: "To download this white paper, email Frank."

"Wait," I said to myself, "who the hell is Frank?"

I could tell from the sophistication of this website that Frank was not an AI bot. This was confirmed when I clicked the button, and, sure enough, it actually opened up my email client to send a message to frank@[company name].com. It kills me that I am not including the screen shot, given this happened in 2018, but I'm too nice (and it's my dad's friend). I stared at the window, a thousand questions running through my head. What did Frank expect me to say? Was there some secret password I had to know in order to gain access to the white paper? Would Frank expect us to be friends afterward?

Ultimately, I'll never know. I simply closed the window and got on with my day.

From a personalization perspective, a setup like this is a mess. For starters, it's inconvenient. Customers should never have to email some random person at a company just to download a white paper. If nothing else, that's what automated (and personalized!) lead capture tools are for.

The worst part, though—and I know nobody at the company intended it this way—is that the whole thing ended up feeling sketchy. Your customers aren't going to want to suffer through an awkward conversation with some guy named Frank. Most of us avoid interactions like that as if our lives depended on it. We just want our white paper so we can carry on with our lives.[18]

Now, to be fair, I'm sure 99 percent of you reading this book are well beyond making this kind of mistake. Your organization probably doesn't have any Franks sitting around jealously guarding the keys to the white paper castle. I use this example not to talk you out of doing something like this, since I assume you're not doing it the first place, but rather to remind you that content experiences this bad really do exist—which makes it all the more necessary that we prioritize our content experience.

The good news is, most of us make at least *some* effort in that direction. For instance, when I get to my room in one of the hotels I regularly stay at, the TV is always set to say, "Greetings, Randy Frisch." It's a nice touch, but these days, that would also be considered bare minimum (like my earlier email example). If they had *really* wanted to impress me, they could have offered a personalized set of

18   In case you were wondering, the answer is no, I did not email Frank to get access to his white paper. I am, however, very curious to know what would happen if I did, and what a conversation with Frank might be like.

recommendations to accommodate me on my business trip. For bonus points, they could have even linked the TV to my Netflix account and had the next episode of my favorite show queued up to watch.

I'm not trying to sound picky here—really, I'm okay with the hotel not doing any of this, for now. However, I know of plenty of other hotels that *do* go that extra mile. For instance, another hotel, Fairmont Hotels, has gone to great lengths to accommodate one of our employees, Paige. Whenever Paige is in town, they have a robe and some green tea ready for her because they know she's going to want them. She hasn't had to ask for either of those small creature comforts since her first visit. As soon as she gets to her room, they're ready and waiting for her.

That's the level all of us should aspire to as marketers. And as the following strategies show, there are plenty of ways to go about doing this in marketing our products and services.

HOW TO PERSONALIZE EXPERIENCES

Personalizing the experience will impact how customers move through the buyer journey, and most importantly, how they view your brand. After organizing content contextually, it's time for the fun part—creating collections and designing an experience around them, like a resource center, email nurture, or ABM campaign. The devil is in the details here; think personalized messaging, custom images, and company branding. By creating a better experience around your content, your prospects and customers are more likely to engage and convert.

INBOUND

When it comes to inbound marketing, personalization comes into play with the content you create. After all, content marketers tend to produce their content based on the challenges and questions relevant to their audience. Then, it's also about distributing that content across paid, owned, and earned channels to engage people and get them back to your site.

In the previous chapter, we talked about the idea that people are looking for content to solve whatever problems they may have. Back in the day, it was enough to simply have content and expect people to dig through your assets until they found something valuable. Those days are gone. Our allegiance to the Netflixes and Googles of the world clearly demonstrate that, these days, we expect a high degree of personalization.

The Alight Way

For starters, we need to make sure our inbound content is

the first result in a search engine or that it's easily surfaced in a social media post. Then it becomes all about the next asset we suggest once we have our customers' attention. It has to be spot-on to their needs if we expect them to continue on their journey with us. We can't expect them to go back to find that next perfect asset. Remember, it's more likely they'll go back to the medium's infinite scroll. We have to hook them into *our* infinite scroll.

One example of a company that does this well is Alight, a leading provider of benefits administration and cloud-based HR solutions. The marketing team at Alight understands that most people don't come to their website to find content by format; they come looking for answers to specific problems. Alight's typical customers come to them because they're working from antiquated HR systems and considering a move to the cloud. However, many aren't entirely sure what this newfangled "cloud" is, which puts the onus on Alight to educate in order to sell.

Alight understands what a huge shift this is for their customers. They know that a single content asset—for instance, a video on how to navigate the talent management landscape—isn't going to be enough to get the average visitor to convert. So, rather than drop their prospects into a single asset, they drop them into a dynamic stream of content that offers a combination of ebooks, videos, and blog posts all geared around a combination of case studies and ROI metrics associated with making the switch to Alight. In other words, they set their visitors up to go down a specific rabbit hole and consume the content necessary to convert them to a qualified lead. Before their visitors even realize it, Alight has set themselves up as the go-to expert in cloud-based HR solutions, all because they masterfully served up a variety of useful inbound information in seconds.

Alight also sells to another persona—health benefit administrators who may not need to spearhead that move to the cloud. Content for this group is a bit different and focused more on understanding how to manage health benefit administration at scale. This type of buyer gets dropped in a different contextual stream.

Marketing to Multiple Buyers

Remember, according to Gartner, 6.8 different buyers—let's just say seven—weigh in on your buying cycle. As marketers, we're never trying to influence only one person, but rather seven. To do that, we need to create personalized streams for discovery at the top of the funnel. Like Alight, we must take each different persona on their own journey. Even if we're marketing on a one-to-many rather than a one-to-one basis, we must still offer the same degree of personalization focused on the specific areas of interest among our different segments.

This is why it's important to centralize your content into a front-facing web experience, as we discussed in chapter 6. From there, you can build out the necessary contextual streams. This helps solve one of the longest-standing questions of inbound marketing: Where does our content live at the end of the day? The answer is in what we've long called a resource center—albeit one reimagined for how our customers actually look for content. In this reimagined resource center (or content hub, knowledge center, or whatever else you want to call it), content is strategically built around the specific personas, industries, and challenges relevant to our audience so they can better evaluate our product or service. In that way, our content becomes adaptive to our many buyers and their different journeys.

Dunk in the Dark Isn't Good Enough

One more thing before we wrap up our discussion of personalization within inbound marketing. It's important to know that as we continue to consider scale and personalization, we may even hit a point in our inbound strategy of having streams of content that aren't on a menu tied to our websites, but rather to a niche area that someone might be searching for.

For instance, take a social strategy where your social media marketer is jumping on top of trending topics. One of my favorite modern campaigns in the consumer world came back in 2013 when, in the middle of the Super Bowl, all the lights went out on the field. A bright marketer at Oreo quickly executed a tweet that referred to the idea that you can still dunk in the dark, regardless of the fact that you can't watch the game in that moment. That tweet received a week's worth of press and earned (as of this writing) 525 million impressions.[19]

Oreo Cookie @Oreo   3 Feb
Power out? No problem. pic.twitter.com/dnQ7pOgC
Hide photo   ← Reply   ⟲ Retweet   ★ Favorite   ••• More

YOU CAN STILL DUNK IN THE DARK

16,059   **6,153**
RETWEETS   FAVORITES

---

19 For a more complete accounting of the famous "dunk in the dark" tweet, see: Jenny Rooney, "Behind the Scenes of Oreo's Real-Time Super Bowl Slam Dunk," *Forbes*, February 4, 2013. https://www.forbes.com/sites/jenniferrooney/2013/02/04/behind-the-scenes-of-oreos-real-time-super-bowl-slam-dunk/-5506f2512e66.

Moments like these are great, but when they happen, marketers should always be thinking about their next move. How could Oreo have taken that opportunity to further immerse us in the brand? Many of us don't think about that next step, but it's a crucial one. To engage customers with more complex buying decisions, we can't depend solely on the trending moment. We must also take the time to capture our audience in an immersive experience that allows them to continue their journey of discovery until they are ready to do business with us.

Again, this is where the Content Experience Framework becomes so important. As long as you have centralized and organized your content so that everything is both accounted for and easily searchable, it becomes easy for your social media manager to jump in and build a spur-of-the-moment content stream in minutes that tells a story and guides prospects through a truly personalized experience.

DEMAND GENERATION

Demand generation is the strategy that so many marketers associate with modern marketing because it spans so many stages of the journey and has a strong impact on buyers' understanding of what a company stands for and, ultimately, how its products and services will tie into someone's requirements. That's why it's so important that we learn to move past the clickbait headline and focus more on the value-add of each asset being dangled.

This isn't accomplished in just one move. Demand generation involves a series of moves to convert and nurture prospects, then continue to support them through the buyer journey. In order to understand how to get personalization *right* in demand generation, we first need to look at what it looks like when it's done wrong.

Nurture Like You Mean It

One common type of personalization fail comes in the form of the email nurtures marketers often send off (just like my experience with Volkswagen back in chapter 1). To be sure, marketers' email nurture game has improved over the years, but we can do better. Many marketers have already moved away from the email-as-newsletter format, where leads would have to read the email, embrace the call-to-action, and then click a link that leads them to some content they can finally engage with.

These days, the more popular approach is to keep things simpler; use email to direct the prospect to a single asset that lives in a native feed or news stream. Again, the problem becomes how to get that prospect to move on to the next personalized asset. If we just drop them into our news feed, they'll simply see the next most-recent post—but as we've already discussed, a chronological approach rarely produces relevant results for the customer. It's not mapped out to their needs or buyer's journey, and therefore, it's difficult to earn their trust as a customer.

To put personalization at the center of your demand generation efforts, send the person to a collection of assets that are all geared around that same campaign that you are speaking to. That way, if the customer wants to self-nurture out of interest, they are able to do it.

Blackbaud, a cloud software company that powers social good, does this very well. At Blackbaud, one of their lead marketers, Lisa Kenney, carefully curates specific content collections and makes sure the design of each one flows all the way through from beginning to end.

This is a smart approach for a company like Blackbaud. "Social good" is a broad category, meaning their team has to serve a variety of markets across the globe—all segmented by product and use. However, because of Lisa and her team's efforts, each email they send out feels personalized, with a specific call-to-action that links to a dedicated stream centered on a specific persona and segment. Again, none of this is organized by content type; sometimes the first asset is a blog, and sometimes it's a video. Whatever the case, once in the stream, the prospect will have plenty of other relevant content to choose from.

Remember, at the end of the day, it's also about providing consistent experiences. By designing your demand generation efforts around dedicated content streams, you're creating controlled environments that drive conversations. Think back to our IKEA example in chapter 1. They don't drop us into their warehouse to shop. Rather, they show us rooms where everything complements each other, giving us comfort. Similarly, it's not just about sending your prospects to a warehouse of content—that's not a great way to earn their trust. Instead, it's about sending them to a collection of assets that are valuable to them on their buyer's journey so they can see the entire picture (or room, if you will).

The Landing Page Minefield

Demand generation marketers also run into trouble when it comes to keywords and paid searches. Depending on the keywords you're targeting, paying for clicks can get pretty expensive. This puts the onus on us as marketers to keep our prospects engaged and clicking through once they get to our landing page, otherwise we're just creating a dead-end experience—and wasting money in the process.

This is certainly a big challenge for many marketers. At the time of this writing, the average conversion rate of a typical landing page is only 2.35 percent.[20] That means 97.65 percent of visitors aren't engaged enough to continue forward on their buyer's journey.

Marketers debate about the reasons for this. A lot of it centers on whether we should send prospects to dead-end landing pages or allow visitors to continue their journey organically if they don't want to convert on that asset. I tend to fall in the latter camp. As long as you provide some structure to the experience, you should absolutely give your prospects the chance to navigate to other relevant content—if for no other reason than it helps build trust over time.

Again, the key here is to focus on personalization. If you're going to let your visitors explore, you surround them with assets that are relevant to them and that encourage them to continue their journey. Some of this means thinking less on conversion and more on engagement. There's nothing wrong with making an offer in order to capture valuable information from your prospects. However, instead of trying to push a free demo, offer something

---

20 Larry Kim, "7 Conversion Rate Truths That Will Change Your Landing Page Strategy," *Search Engine Land,* May 15, 2014, https://searchengineland. com/7-conversion-rate-truths-will-change-landing-page-optimization-strategy-191083.

with a little less commitment and more top-of-funnel value, like a blog post or something along those lines.

Not everyone is going to agree with me on this, and that's okay. Some of you are committed to your landing pages, and you only want to attract people who are ready to convert before you let them browse. Still, let's be clear on what needs to happen post-conversion. After they get that ebook or that free demo, they still might not be ready to make a purchase. In that case, how do you keep moving them through the buyer's journey? What's the next step? Whatever you decide on, make sure you decide on something. It would be a shame if, after all that hard work getting your prospects to convert on your landing page, you're stuck waiting for your prospect to bring themselves back into the funnel on their own.

To that end, here's a tip: optimize your thank-you page. Keep the engagement going. Don't stop at "Thanks for giving us your information. Here's a link to that report." Follow that report up with six other pieces of content centered on that topic. Make sure that you design every element of the paid ad/landing page/lead capture process to continue seamlessly into the email nurture you're sure to drop them into afterward.

Track Everything

To make personalization work in your demand generation strategy, it's important that you track engagement. This way, you know exactly what assets lead someone down the various end points to purchase—which in turn allows you to better personalize similar experiences down the road. Advanced tracking usually requires some combination of analytical tools like Google Analytics, and as you scale, you'll likely want to track more of those activities back to your marketing automation platform.

A focus on tracking data not only allows you to demonstrate the real value of your demand programs and fueling pipeline, but also to better understand how your customers consume the content to self-nurture them through the journey faster.

ACCOUNT-BASED MARKETING

As we touched on in chapter 4, ABM is very much about landing the accounts your team considers to be the best fit for your organization. But simply selecting the right accounts doesn't mean they'll come running to you. As much as people focus on the planning stages of selecting and tiering the right accounts, the real key is in how to actually land those accounts. It's on marketers to engage those accounts—and here once again, content takes center stage.

The scary part about ABM is thinking about how to personalize content at scale and then distribute it to individual accounts. According to Forrester, 95 percent of marketers say that personalization and engagement is the key to ABM success.[21] Unfortunately, according to that same survey, 39 percent of marketers struggled to personalize their content for specific accounts, and 38 percent struggled with getting those accounts to engage in their content.

The key here is leveraging the organization and centralization of content to give teams the ability to pull the right content for the right accounts with ease. Each account has different needs, but in order to scale, you'll need to be able to automate the process using whatever tagging and organizational structure you've put in place. From there, you can take the extra steps necessary to make sure your branding efforts are customized—your logo is there, your messaging is speaking directly to the target account, and you lay out a clear plan for the potential issues you can solve for.

Proving ROI Account by Account

Remember Daniel from Snowflake and the streams he

---

21   Forrester, "Not Yet the New Normal: ABM Must Evolve into Account-Based Engagement," June 29, 2018, https://www.forrester.com/report/Not+Yet+The+New+Normal+ABM+Must+Evolve+Into+AccountBased+Engagement/-/E-RES118049.

was building to engage target accounts? Here's what he did: each account received a page of content that was sent to them through a variety of different demand generation techniques that felt personalized with things like a message to them, their logo, and most importantly, content assets that were relevant to their sector.

With executive approval to secure a CEP, they were armed to scale those first twelve account streams to three hundred, each with their very own personal stream of content. They set a new standard inside the company that helped differentiate them from the competition.

Each of those accounts requires microsites and streams of content. Daniel uses these as part of his entire integrated marketing campaign. He leverages retargeted ads to accounts that they want to land by using solutions like Terminus, where they have their logo and the company's logo in a united fashion. They make sure that when someone clicks that ad, the same degree of personalization is met on the flipside. Daniel says, "Our reps can email someone a hundred times and phone them twenty times. But if a prospect gets a display ad directing them to a stream of content that is personalized to them, they are blown away."

What's great about Daniel's story is the success he saw in the early days by hacking these microsites together for key accounts. Daniel has since won multiple marketing awards for his approach to ABM, personalization, and a focus on content experience.

SALES ENABLEMENT

Throughout the book, I've stressed the importance of marketing taking ownership of the entire buyer journey. A marketer's job does not end at the lead, let alone MQL. They need to continue generating demand and supporting the pipeline. In order to truly be successful, your sales and marketing must be aligned.[22] After all, at the end of the day, the sales department is often just as responsible for delivering content assets to prospects as marketing is.

Sales Reps Aren't Content Creators

We've all seen sales teams going off and creating their own content rather than using the assets marketing has provided them with. We love our sales reps (seriously, we really do), but they tend to be more casual with the content they produce or curate. They don't obsess over consistency the way marketers do.

Have you ever spent months working on a slide deck for a really important sales presentation, only for that content to get spun out into fifty different—and conflict-

---

22 For those of you who don't know the lingo, this is often referred to as *smarketing*.

ing—pieces of content by the sales team? Their hearts are in the right place, but something is lost in the translation. It's kind of like getting information from the last kid in line during a game of broken telephone. It's cute when the kids do it and say something incoherent at the end, but when the sales rep has manipulated well-thought-out messaging and strategy that a marketing team specifically designed, the last thing that's heard is laughter or profanity.

Every minute a sales rep spends creating content is a minute they're not selling. If they're manipulating all these assets because they don't understand what marketing has already created for them, they're just wasting valuable minutes. This time *should* be spent pitching or coming up with a good strategy for positioning the marketing-approved content they've been provided.

The Google Trap

One of the things I've observed over the years by watching sales reps at different companies—including those that I've overseen—is that, when they're looking for company-related content, they go to a very logical (but very scary) place: Google. Again, to many this would seem logical. Sure, Google indexes content well, but they do it over time, not necessarily by what is most relevant in the moment and to a specific audience. Such an approach makes the sales team great at finding an old PDF that used to be helpful, but it's unlikely that PDF is aligned to your integrated marketing campaign for this month, this week, or even this day.

It's hard to personalize content when you're working from dated materials. Many sales reps also have a "tried, tested, and true" template email that they send to every prospect they come across. Forget personas, forget the six curated pieces of content, forget anything that might earn trust with our prospects. Everyone gets the same assets, whether they like it or not.

I'm painting a grim picture here, but I want to be clear that the sales team doesn't deserve the blame for this. When you're not sure where else to find your own branded content, why *wouldn't* you turn to Google? It's our job as marketers to arm our sales reps with content that they can personalize on the fly—and we do that by building a content hub packed to the brim with all the content we own. That way, all they have to do is head to the hub, perform the same kind of search they would on Google, and then plug the right assets into their sales process.

Be the Solution

Engaging an enterprise-level client can often take six months to a year or more. It's a lot to ask of your sales reps to search through every email they've ever sent to remember what asset they sent their prospect and when—and the more you scale your business, the more this becomes a challenge. This is where a dedicated CEP comes in handy. Such a platform allows you to create dedicated sales streams for your team—just like Terminus did.

The key with personalization in sales enablement is to arm salespeople with a destination or content experience that is truly one-to-one, so it feels like a connection between the sales rep and the target prospects. That way, prospective customers have a reliable place to turn to once the sales call is over. They can look over that presentation the sales team just walked them through without having to search through a bunch of emails to find it.

The final piece of this, of course, is communication. Make sure your sales reps understand all the content they have available to them, what its purpose is, and most importantly, how they can access it. By doing so, you're setting them up for success, allowing them to build personalized content experiences for their clients and manage the sales cycle better in the process.

THE FINAL WORD ON PERSONALIZATION

As you think through these four approaches and consider how you might build your own team's go-to-market strategy, consider whether you are building a destination that is as engaging as an afternoon on Netflix, or whether you're sending people off to a dead end. In the personalization phase, this is where you begin to take a step back, examine your buyer journey, and consider the marketing tactics you are using at each step. From there, the question is, what experiences do you need at each stage to complement the process?

Hopefully, this chapter hasn't overwhelmed you too much, because now comes the fun part. This is where you get to create the memorable experiences. You may not be at the stage of nailing your inbound, demand generation, ABM, and sales enablement today, but pick one area to focus on. Prove that it works and then continue to build out.

We've found that our dedication to personalization has made all the difference in our go-to-market strategy at Uberflip. It may be an anecdotal example, but the most meaningful evidence that these efforts work is the response we get from our audience. Instead of ignoring us, they engage. They send us messages. They share our content. They comment on our posts. They share their experiences with us and how much it meant to them.

Little things like this make us feel valued as marketers. Our team never gets sick of seeing responses like this because it allows us to see that all our hard work mapping content out and creating positive experiences for people is actually paying off.

By focusing on creating positive experiences, your team can build the same kind of trust with your audience. And once you have that trust, that audience will open up the privacy gates and begin engaging with you on a regular basis. Eventually, even the skeptics like Jay will learn to trust your brand.

CHAPTER 9

DISTRIBUTE

___

As CMO, I like to get copies of what we're sending to our subscribers to make sure we're drinking our own champagne. Some time ago, I received a weekly content roundup email from our own company that gave us a rude awakening. The email contained a link to a video, which was good, but after clicking around, I noticed there were no CTAs accompanying some of our podcasts. As I clicked through to the hub, I found competing CTAs, links that went to different unrelated topics, and if I'm being honest, a lackluster (and not well-thought-out) experience.

So what went wrong? In short, our content wasn't mapped out properly—not a good look for a company focused on content experience, but at least it was a good learning opportunity. If we were going to help other brands do this, we had to own the content experience within our own walls, too. From there, we began to develop a whole framework to make sure that every asset had a purpose, a clear call-to-action, and a specific stage within the buyer journey.

Rude awakenings like this happen in all companies. In the early days of Uberflip, we obsessed over the content experience. Our content strategy was top-notch. Yet, in creating all this great content, we took our eye off of what was important: owning the experience at every stage of our journey. Once we recognized our error, we were able to challenge ourselves back into doing things the correct way.

We learned the hard way that every step of the Content Experience Framework needed equal attention if it was going to work. We'd done great with the first three steps of the process (centralize, organize, and personalize), but when it came to the next phase (distribute), we had dropped the ball.

A lot of it came down to a mindset shift. We realized that we needed to think about distribution not as something you address once a quarter, but rather as something you address *every day*. Somewhere along the way, we'd lost sight of this, and the result was complete disorganization, both internally and externally for the audience we were trying to engage.

I've said it earlier in this book, and I'll say it again: creating good content isn't good enough. We need a great experience. If you don't have a strong distribution plan, people won't find your personalized destinations on their own. After all, many of them are truly personalized one-to-one, so they're not meant to be *found*. In this chapter, just like I did with my own team after opening that email and seeing what a mess we'd created, I challenge you to step up and own your distribution game.

DISTRIBUTION IN THE MODERN AGE

The term distribution has been used in so many different ways by marketers over the years. If you go back to the four Ps, one of them was *place*, but it could just as easily be called distribution, since both involve how we take our offering to the market. These days, it's not quite as simple as one method or direct path. To capture the attention of our audience, we need to create an omnichannel presence for our brand.

As you're no doubt aware, today's consumer doesn't go to one location to make their decision. They navigate across a variety of channels—social media, review sites, online merchants, etc.—and marketers have to meet them at every touchpoint. For example, say you're sending an email. A lot of people just think about simply plugging in a single content asset when they could be linking to a curated experience that leads customers through that golden number of seven pieces of content—all in one email.

To use another example, consider social media. When it comes to platforms like Twitter, Facebook, or LinkedIn, how does your marketing team usually share content? Most likely, you simply grab the URL built off of your homepage, plug it into the post, and that's that. Just like with email, here's an excellent opportunity to strategically build out an experience. Customize that asset so that it drops your audience into a targeted content stream. If you've done your due diligence in the first three steps of our framework, then the additional work in this step is minimal.

In the last chapter, I mentioned Oreo's brilliant tweet that a clever marketer sent out during that infamous power outage during the 2013 Super Bowl. It was a great moment, but also a missed opportunity. Imagine if Oreo had taken that experience further, linking people to a fun stream dedicated to all the different ways and situations you could dunk an Oreo. A clever campaign is great— but a clever campaign tied to six other similar assets is even better.

WHO IS IN CHARGE OF DISTRIBUTION?

Before we go any further, let's talk about roles. A lot of times, we think that content marketers simply create the content and then hand it off to the demand generation team to push it out. The problem is, if you silo these roles too much and don't put the two teams in conversation with each other, that's when the poor experiences occur, because we fail to give the natural opportunity to convert or continue down a path.

I suspect that's what happened with that email I opened up that fateful day at Uberflip. The content team had written a specific piece designed for a specific part of the buyer journey. However, because there wasn't enough communication between teams, demand generation simply grabbed the asset because they liked it and plunked it into the email they were sending out.

This works in the other direction as well. The content marketer needs to understand the journey that the demand generation team wants to send their audience down so they can build out content to reflect that path. It's a crucial aspect of the journey, but if your teams are siloed, it's all but impossible to think about your experience from end to end. The result is a chaotic experience for the end user—and a loss of whatever trust you may have built up.

HOW TO UP YOUR DISTRIBUTION GAME

At this point, you may be saying to yourself, *How am I possibly going to personalize or distribute these unique experiences in all my different tactics?* No doubt, you'll have plenty to consider when it comes to distribution. That's why the other steps of our Content Experience Framework are so important. Put in the work at each step, and you'll be well-equipped for the distribution stage because all your personalized experiences will be ready to go.

If you don't, you'll find yourself stuck in a reactionary loop. You'll be searching for a single content asset on an as-needed basis, day in and day out. That approach can certainly bring limited success, but more likely, it's putting a cramp on your conversion rate. It's sending leads on dead-end paths rather than on tailor-made buyer journeys.

No one wants that. So, to help you understand what I mean, let's take a look at how to up your distribution game within the context of a few different tactics, including some tactics my team has deployed with success.

EMAIL

When nurturing leads through an email campaign, we often organize our content by buyer persona. Then, we build out a nurture campaign around this content, carefully considering the different stages of the buyer's journey and what that might look like. At each stage, we greet the lead with an experience that's carefully aligned with our goals. Because this content has already been mapped out by its stage, organizing the content for email becomes a snap.

Let's dissect this further in context of one of our target personas. If our buyer persona enters our sales funnel at the top, we have a series of content assets that will resonate at that stage. Depending on their level of engagement, subsequent emails will move this buyer to different experiences that match that level.

With every message, we use the same articles that the buyer could have found somewhere else (i.e., social media, a resource center, etc.). However, there's a slight— but important—difference. The content may largely be the same, but the CTAs our persona sees are specifically contextualized to match where they are on the buyer journey. Instead of a generic experience, this buyer gets a highly tailored experience that's perfectly tuned to their particular nurture program. Then, with every stage and every piece of content they engage with, we have more data to contextualize their next stage in the path and adjust accordingly.

Again, this might sound like a lot to put into action, but

if you've built out these experiences ahead of time—whether by persona, topic, or account—then mapping those experiences to your nurture campaign can be as easy as a few clicks; all the setup is done ahead of time. Further, such an approach allows the prospect the freedom to self-nurture. All you have to do is present them with a path and let them decide how to follow it.

Blackbaud, who we mentioned earlier, has taken this approach to the next level. Not only have they built out these wonderfully designed experiences to map to their buyers' journeys, but they have also infused artificial intelligence into the process in the form of a content recommendation engine. The second they detect a prospect who is really engaging with their nurture campaigns, the recommendation engine kicks in with helpful suggestions and increases the buyer's pipeline velocity.

Although we've focused a lot of our examples on personalization, in terms of environment, structure, and engagement, campaigns like this exhibit all the essential aspects of a good content experience:

1. The environment is well-thought-out because it's wrapped in a great experience. Time is put into building an environment that is visually appealing, is easy to navigate, and has a clear message.
2. The structure is aligned to specific stages of the buyer

journey, as well as the persona that the content is tied to.

3. The engagement is strengthened with specific, targeted CTAs that are contextualized to the content in that stage through a recommendation engine.

With me so far? Great. Let's take a look at a few more examples, since, after all, we're not just living in a world of email.

PAID ADS

When working with paid ads, many marketers simply send prospective buyers to a landing page and cross their fingers that they will convert. As we said last chapter, the sad reality is that only 2.35 percent of those people who get to the landing page actually do. Part of the reason so many people leave is because they aren't given a journey to discover and learn from. If we take the same idea of putting someone through a personalized experience, then we can put up more strategic locations for them to convert. We can even give them the opportunity to discover more content if they're not ready to do so. Through some of the work we've done at my company with customers craving a better content experience, we saw more fluid pop-up calls-to-action put the conversion rate around 17 percent on average compared to that 2.35 percent. That's over seven times better.

Now, I'm not suggesting that there is no place for landing pages if we're trying to get someone to sign up for or buy a product. Especially with a more transactional product, the landing page may be the better option. However, when we're trying to educate, we need to remember that landing pages are not necessarily built for gating content. They were built for A/B testing conversion pages.

To that end, here's my recommendation: use landing pages to convert that initial lead and begin your buyer's journey, not to close the deal. If you're spending money on getting someone to click on a paid ad and you drop them into a piece of content, you should not evaluate success based on whether they click through on that ad or read just the first piece of content. Focus on what they did after that. Where did they go versus where you wanted them to go?

DIRECT MAIL

With the rise of ABM, direct mail is suddenly cool again. Many marketers are leveraging personalized packages with meaningful gifts to get the attention of their buyers. For instance, companies like PFL help marketers send carefully curated boxes of goodies to future and current customers.

On our end at Uberflip, we launched a chatbot on our

website that qualifies visitors with an icebreaker question. If a target account engages with the bot, it asks the question, "Are you more into music or movies?" If the person answers, "I'm a movie lover," and if we already have other information from them like physical address, we send them a Netflix direct mail package. If they answer, "I am a music lover," we send a Spotify package.

Inside the Netflix box will be a bag of popcorn and Skittles so that our prospective customers can binge their favorite TV shows and movies and have a good time on us. It also includes a call-to-action to do one of two things:

1. Book a demo with us and get $100 on Netflix.
2. Head straight to a custom URL with content geared specifically toward their role within the company.

Demand Gen

You're a master of orchestrating demand generation. But are you capable of quickly spinning up custom content experiences (like this one) for target audiences to drive deeper, more personalized engagement? To learn more about how our platform can transform your campaigns and conversions with content, book a demo and we'll give you $100 in Netflix.

Depending on whether you're taking a one-to-one, one-to-few, or one-to-many approach, and how important an account is, the custom landing page you send your target account to may go beyond simply targeting a persona and have even more information specific to their account.

THE LAST WORD ON DISTRIBUTION

Way back toward the beginning of this book, I told you all about my great love for Spotify and how great it is at queuing up or recommending the exact music my son Ethan and I want to hear when we're on the road and headed to a hockey game.

No one does personalization like Spotify, because Spotify understands that personalization is made real to their customers through top-notch distribution. To a buyer like me, "Made for Randy" aren't just hollow words. They're a promise that what I'm about to listen to really is curated to me and my specific tastes.

At Uberflip, if we didn't learn our lesson after our email debacle, we have now. Every time I open Spotify, I'm reminded of the importance of not just designing but also *delivering* personalized experiences to our audience wherever they are in the buyer journey.

The last question is, how do you know if your efforts have worked? We'll tackle that answer in the next chapter, the final step of our Content Experience Framework.

CHAPTER 10

GENERATE RESULTS

—

In the early days of the company, as much as I am a marketer at heart, I sometimes had to put my sales hat on. This is true for any (co)founder who's tasked with figuring out whether the ideas that they're trying to bring to market are actually going to work. It was while wearing this sales hat that I met Heather, a marketing vet with over thirty years of experience, through a warm referral. I was excited to hear her take on the content experience and how she thought it might bolster her content marketing efforts.

She was more than willing to share her opinion: "I have no interest in content marketing. It's a waste of time and resources. I only took this call because it's a referral."

Well, at least she was being honest. I took a deep breath and thought to myself, *This is going to be a fun call.*

And it was. Even if she had no interest in what I was selling, I realized I had a great learning opportunity in front of me to understand what I was up against as a marketer. So, rather than get defensive, I simply said, "You know what, you've been doing marketing for twenty years more than me. Why don't you tell me about some of the times content marketing let you down. Give me all your war stories."

She was more than excited to unload, and soon I had a clear picture of where her distrust for content marketing stemmed from. Heather, it turned out, had been an early adopter. She and her team had experimented with content marketing before it was a buzzword—and before marketers had the ability to map a path and track engagement. *Of course* she felt the way she did. Without ever being able to prove that content marketing could actually generate results, why would she think otherwise?

UNDERSTANDING THE PATH TO GOOD RESULTS

A bit of a disclaimer, if you will, to the framework here. The generate results step isn't something that you do at the end of a process or that magically just happens where we sit back and see the money pour in while we drink our Coronas. It's more of a mindset that we need to focus on at every stage. If we do, then at the end we should see impactful results. At every stage we've explored, from centralizing to personalizing, we've been noting little and big process changes to set ourselves up for a result-oriented outcome. As we put together the framework a while back, we debated whether *results* should be something that surrounded all four steps or existed as step five. In the end, we felt it was important to include it as its own step at the end, to remind us that our goal with content is to generate results that impact the growth and success of our organization.

In this chapter, we're absolutely going to talk about how to leverage content experience to produce relevant, meaningful results. However, before we do, here's another story from my early days as a marketer that helped shape my entire mindset as a results-driven marketer.

My first job out of university was at a company called Newell Rubbermaid, which most people know for their totes and sandwich boxes. I was super excited to be hired as a *field marketing rep*, which I naively assumed was going to be all about *marketing*. The job was ultimately about sales. I shuffled from Walmart to Walmart in a certain region of Ontario, Canada, and was responsible for making sure products were shipped and presented in the store in a way that encouraged people to buy. We kiddingly referred to ourselves as glorified traveling stock boys/girls.

Three months in, I was asked to build an in-aisle display in the parking lot of a store because the store manager told me I was taking up too much space in the back room. While constructing the cardboard structure from the equivalent of a bunch of Lego pieces, a big wind swept through and blew all the cardboard parts across the parking lot. At that moment, I remember thinking to myself, *I'm going home and quitting today. I didn't go to school and get a degree to do this.* I threw a few more swear words out into that biting wind, recovered all my "Lego pieces," and finished the job (after a call with my dad calmed me down).

The first thing I did when I got home was call one of my mentors so I could share my misery with someone. They weren't having it.

"What you have to remember right now is that you're seeing how results are generated. You're seeing at the store level what works and what doesn't. If you want a marketing role with more responsibility, where you're able to build and ship products, think about the context you're getting here at the store level."

I took these words to heart, and roughly a year later, I was promoted into a product marketing role and quickly realized how right my mentor was. That opportunity in the stores had provided me with context of what did and didn't work at a store level that some people with five years of experience still didn't understand. They had never done that job and had never seen the buyer journey path on the floor. It taught me the importance of taking the time to understand the path that someone goes through when buying—and what results are important on the road to earning that person's business.

CAPTURE THE LEAD

Content marketing gets a bad rap because it's often seen as an expense as opposed to an investment that generates revenue. To change our company's view, we need to get very tactical—not to mention tactful—about what happens next when someone starts down a path of consuming content. The challenge here is overcoming the tendency to place the same two or three CTAs across our content, somewhat the same way we do across our website. How do we tie the right CTA in to get the desired response and generate results?

Throughout this book, we've talked about the importance of contextualizing your CTAs to the appropriate moment in the buyer journey. To show that your investment in the content experience was worth it, your CTAs must capture real, marketing-qualified leads that you can pass on to your sales team. At minimum, this means collecting the right data and having a scoring model in place to accelerate the more enthusiastic, self-nurturing leads through the sales funnel faster.

Fortunately, we marketers (unlike Heather at the time) have an array of marketing automation platforms and CRM tools that can help us track engagement, score leads, and gain insights on our various content assets. Now, depending on your strategy—be it inbound, demand generation, ABM, or sales enablement—you're going to focus on different insights to get you there. For instance, an inbound approach is largely driven by persona, whereas an ABM approach is driven by specific data about your target accounts. Whatever approach you're taking, your driving question should be: how can you design an experience that engages your target buyer while allowing you to gain the insights you need to move them forward?

TRACKING PERFORMANCE

Remember, the Content Experience Framework is not about creating content. It's about how we structure and distribute that content to generate demand, revenue, and relationships. To that end, some of your content will be a star player, with a direct role in whatever results you're seeking, and some will play more of a supporting role.

I remember trying to explain to my youngest son Ryan when he was six years old the value of passing the puck versus scoring on every rush he had in hockey. Now, Ryan is pretty good with the puck (and was six as I said), so that was a complex idea to unpack. As he put it, "Isn't it just about scoring? If we score more, we win, right?"

I broke it down slowly for him. "Before you scored, how did you get the puck?"

His first answer was obviously to steal it. But eventually I got to explain that at times he got the puck through a pass, which led to many of those goals. It hit home when I referenced that Wayne Gretzky, #99, was not just known as the Great One for his 894 career goals, but his 1,963 assists.

Many of us over-obsess with the asset that converted or "scored the goal." But as we've discussed throughout the Content Experience Framework—we will score more goals revenue if we create a journey (of passes, if you will). The content that assists in that journey is equally important to note and track. This is why many of us have gone beyond tracking the first or last touch to acknowledge the importance of multi-touch attribution. Knowing the difference will help you understand what type of content you should create and place in order to address a specific need or moment in the buyer journey.

At the generate results step in the framework, you need

to showcase how your experiences impact pipeline and revenue—ultimately proving the ROI of your investment in content experience. As you capture leads and data throughout all your content experiences and pass them through to your marketing automation platform, your next step must be to implement a lead-scoring model to effectively track how your prospects are engaging.

LEAD SCORING TIER SYSTEM

DEMOGRAPHIC SCORES AND BEHAVIOR
SCORES BUCKETED INTO 3 LEVELS

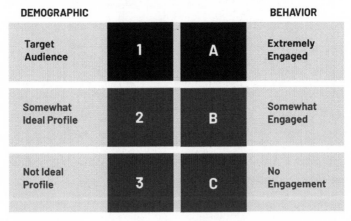

DEMOGRAPHIC			BEHAVIOR
Target Audience	1	A	Extremely Engaged
Somewhat Ideal Profile	2	B	Somewhat Engaged
Not Ideal Profile	3	C	No Engagement

EACH LEVEL IS BROKEN DOWN BASED ON POINTS

I am not going to unpack this for you (a quick Google search will give you plenty of how-to-lead-scoring models), but I thought it would be helpful to show you the model my team uses to score content. We use a tiering system based on demographic and behavior scores to ensure we're only sending the right prospects over to sales at the time they're most engaged.

Understanding this will help to ensure you're passing (not to be confused with my hockey analogy) leads to sales at that exact right moment.

As prospects make their way through this journey, by using a CEP and attribution tools (we use a combo of Uberflip, Bizible, and Domo), you will begin to see patterns as more and more prospects interact with the tailor-made experiences you've created at each stage. You'll uncover key insights like what content drives prospects to that next step of the journey and which assets are page-turners or page-bouncers. This will set you up to be able to build the perfect journey for your buyers that's not only personalized, but also impacts the bottom line.

My team continually tracks how the content experiences we produce influence pipeline and revenue. As you can see in the high-level chart below, tracking the metrics outlined at each stage of the sales funnel sets our team up to stay nimble when content isn't hitting the mark, which ensures we reach our quarterly sales targets.

Attract	Convert	Close
Sessions	Ideal Account Profile Lead Fit	Assets Downloaded / Viewed at Each Opp Stage
Session Duration	Average Content Assets Per Session	Return Visit Rate by SQLs
Clicks	Content Assists (Page visit directly before conversion)	Content Multi-Touch Attribution
Click-Through Rate (CTR)	CTR of Email Nurtures	Number of Influenced Opportunities
Bounce Rate	Marketing Qualified Leads (MQL)	Percentage of Opportunities With Content as a Touchpoint
Time on Page	Sales Accepted Leads (SAL)	Influenced Pipeline (Total deal size and asset attribution)
Page views	Sales Qualified Leads (SQL)	Influenced Revenue (Total deal size and asset attribution)
Leads	Content First Touch Attribution	First-Touch Content to Close Ratio
Cost Per Lead for Content	Average Lead Score	Closed-Won With Content Attribution

WIN AND REPEAT

This final aspect of generating results is often the one that's top of mind for most marketers: getting a customer to the point where they make a purchase or continue to buy. For each of the considerations discussed in this chapter, but especially here, this is where you will need to bring the full force of the content experience to bear.

A company called aPriori is a good example of this. Some time ago, the people at aPriori, an enterprise product cost management platform, knew their content experience was subpar—at least, they suspected it was. With no way to gather insights or prove what assets were or weren't working, they had no sense of the value their content was creating for their business.

Eventually, aPriori invested in a CEP, created a dedicated content hub, and spun up tailored experiences for their visitors. Soon, all their metrics began to shoot up:

- Page views increased by 90 percent.
- Pages per visit increased by 137 percent.
- Thirty-two percent of visitors would work through all the content in the hub and then navigate back to the main site to learn more.

Once aPriori had all these insights, they were able to shift their content strategy and focus on momentum. By knowing what content and which experiences were performing, they were able to focus on what was working. All of this enabled aPriori to convert engaged visitors into customers—and later, into enthusiastic advocates.

SOMETIMES IT'S ABOUT THE BRAND

A superstar marketer named Amanda Todorovich spoke at my company's conference, Conex: The Content Experience, in one of its first years. Amanda works at the Cleveland Clinic where they create a lot of great content, but their goal isn't necessarily conversion all the time. When she told me this, I was confused. Instead, the Cleveland Clinic is more focused on building their brand, making the destination an essential content hub, and leveraging it to generate ad revenue to offset cost. She explained that her competition wasn't other hospitals or clinics. Instead, they saw their main competitor as WebMD. As such, their goal was to build a page where they could simply elevate their brand as a thought leader.

Their CTAs did not direct visitors to their services, but rather to their partners (who actually paid for the promotion). This strategy added authority to the content destination by their mere presence. I drop this example to remind us that not all content experiences have a goal of conversion to lead or revenue. Despite this, the game remains the same—engage the visitor, and put them on a path to deepen their engagement through recommendations, all wrapped up in a visually enticing package.

A SIDE NOTE ON CONTENT CREATION

I know I said this book was not written for content marketers at the start. Well, this short paragraph kind of is. As we start to generate results and see what content succeeds in guiding our buyers through their journey, we start to realize what content is kickass, what content is useless, and what content is missing. This data can inform our content creation process, our editorial calendar, and what we invest in as that next blog post, video, ebook, and so on.

THE FINAL WORD ON GENERATING RESULTS

Until recently, the ROI of content was hard to track, leading people like Heather to wave content marketing off entirely as an inherent waste of time and money. However, by focusing on the results-driven aspects discussed here, your organization *will* be able to gather insights that will help you create better content experiences that map to the different stages of the buyer journey.

The trick, then, is knowing your buyer and journey inside and out. In Part II, we stressed the importance of aligning your content experience to your go-to-market strategy of choice. The ultimate goal is to create opportunities and generate revenue. As marketers, we can never lose sight of this goal; without results, you'll soon find yourself without budget, and, even worse, a job! By focusing on your content's environment, structure, and how your audience is compelled to engage, you'll begin to see content reach its full potential, perform the way it was intended, and prove the ROI of your content marketing.

At the end of the day, to prove the value of content marketing, we need full organizational buy-in—from the CMO and CEO all the way down to the summer intern. In Part III, we'll show you how it's done.

PART III

OWNING THE CONTENT EXPERIENCE

Now we're in the home stretch. Hopefully at this point, you're thinking *I know how to get this done. I'm ready to roll.* Great, I love your enthusiasm.

However, before you run out and start creating your own content experiences, the question still remains: how do we accomplish this at scale, and who's going to own it within the marketing team—or even within the organization at large? If you're the CEO, do you just tell the CMO to get it done and hope for the best? If you're the CMO, do you know where you're going to get started and who you're going to put in charge of building out memorable content experiences?

It's a big question, and ultimately the answer is that everybody has a stake in implementing the Content Experience Framework. So, whoever you are reading this book, get ready to take ownership and start focusing on buy-in. It's time to bring content experience to the masses.

CHAPTER 11

ORGANIZATIONAL ALIGNMENT

———

Content marketers (using the busted definition) have enough on their hands simply creating the content. Here's the part where we teach you how to take the burden off your poor, bogged-down content marketers and bring your entire organization together to create compelling, top-to-bottom content experiences.

Back in 2012, when we first founded Uberflip, we had a visual representation of content pulsing through the org (the figure) that attempted to map out how we saw responsibility for the content experience filtering through our ranks. In it, we had a strategic marketing person at the top, with various other people from marketing reporting in. From there, the chart mapped down to other key roles in seemingly unrelated departments—HR, billing, IT, you name it. We knew then that, because everybody in your organization ultimately both creates and relies on content, the responsibility for a good content experience must fall on all of us.

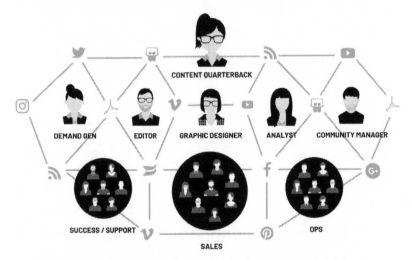

CONTENT QUARTERBACK

DEMAND GEN · EDITOR · GRAPHIC DESIGNER · ANALYST · COMMUNITY MANAGER

SUCCESS / SUPPORT · SALES · OPS

Note: This is the actual image, and our current view is a bit more evolved, but we wanted to keep it real here.

CONTENT IS EVERYONE'S RESPONSIBILITY

You cannot and will not stop people from creating content. Whether it's an email, a website, or people linking you to an article they've found on the internet, it's all content. Nothing is contained to just marketing—and definitely not to just content marketers. Seriously, if at any point throughout this book you've walked over to your content marketing team and said, "Go solve content experiences and align every step through every journey throughout our entire organization," go turn back around and apologize. You got the wrong message. This isn't on the content marketer.

In nearly every organization, every single person working there is leveraging content in one way or another. Sales teams send out content through the emails they write or the links they send out. Customer success or account management teams are often building decks to walk through your product, use cases, or recapping customer stories, but end up describing your solution or go-to-market in a way that may vary from your goals as an organization. The HR team may be advertising roles in your company, including what your company does in job posts that set the wrong expectations. The billing team might be sending out emails that cause customers to have terrible experiences, ruining the connection to them on a regular cadence.

The point is, the organizations that are extremely coordinated in terms of their messaging and their content can actually deliver meaningful experiences regardless of role or department. Some companies already do this very well. Take Slack and Mailchimp, for example. Like many of us, both of these companies need to send out invoices. Except when they do, they inject a combination of a narrative and data. Normally, I don't even look at how much I'm being charged (in fact, I try to look away), but their invoices always catch my attention, because they give me context for how they're helping my organization accomplish its goals. They have mastered a combination of admin, storytelling, and experience.

Companies like this understand that the content experience is expansive. Yet, a lot of us still suffer like the kids playing broken telephone syndrome (see chapter 8). The chain of communication from what a marketer tells a salesperson, to a success person, to a billing person, can break down and create disjointed messaging. The difference between what is said at the beginning and what actually comes out in the end would almost be laughable—except this is our brand message we're talking about, and we definitely don't want that getting diluted.

As we joked in chapter 8, there's never one sales deck for a whole sales team, but rather one deck for each member of the sales team. Each person's spin on the same email ends up creating a Franken-piece of copy-pasted content, dead-end experiences, and mixed messaging. For the rest of this chapter, we're going to talk about how to align the different departments within your organization, who may for the greater good or dire necessity feel the need to own the content experience. There are many groups where we see this in our organizations, but for the purpose of this example, we'll use sales (both pre-sale and post-sale) to illustrate this. Then, in the next chapter, we'll talk about who in the marketing team should own the content experience to bring it all together.

PRE-SALE CONTENT EXPERIENCE

In the sales department, many people try to grab ownership of content and the experience. Often it's the reps, whether they're business or sales development representatives, or account executives, who are crafting emails, follow-ups, and engaging people on every channel, including LinkedIn. Other times it's the sales enablement managers who are crafting and optimizing messaging to be used by those groups. You may even find that sales is so strategic in your organization that it's the VP of sales who decides what deck should be used and what slide should be put where to walk a prospective buyer through the company's narrative.

The reality is, with so many different cooks in the kitchen, we shouldn't be shocked that we end up with that *broken telephone syndrome* inside our organizations. For this reason, it's crucial to identify the right point of contact to interface with marketing to ensure that messaging is aligned from beginning to end.

Let's say, for example, that your marketing team did a great job aligning content on the homepage with messaging that led to a pitch of an offering. I can't tell you how many times I sit through demos where the sales reps try to bring in a new narrative or analogy that clashes with the original one. It may be cute in its own right, but it is far from the style and description of the value that's been outlined until that stage. From there, it only gets worse.

Even in my own company four years ago, I started to hear rumblings of sales reps all having their own versions of our sales deck. We decided to run a strategy session where we took a half-day and had each rep come into the room and walk us through the deck. What we found was that everyone had a different approach—even down to what platform they would use to present the deck. Some would use PowerPoint, while others would use Google Slides (one even cleverly hacked our own platform to work for presenting slides), but each would have different versions of our original slides and different stories of what someone could take away after that call.

Some of you might be asking, "Yeah, but what does this have to do with content or experience?" Well, the reality is that this *is* content—the decks are content, the stories are content, and everything shared after the discovery call is content. And as we said, whenever someone encounters your content, they encounter your content experience. Depending on which sales rep a prospective Uberflip customer got, they were getting an entirely different content experience.

The question was, what should we do about it? At any organization, your sales team is important, and you should do everything you can to empower them in the sales process. However, certain decisions should not be left up to them. If your reps are allowed to change new things that they may not fully understand, they will. You can't blame them, of course; they're simply looking at it from their own experience and the angles that they feel have worked. If they don't know the things that the marketing department knows through research and data, they're not going to stick to what you tell them.

Again, this isn't to say that sales reps shouldn't be allowed any variations in their approach or be given the ability to customize and personalize. A lot of this book is about personalizing, after all, and I'd contradict my own message if I said that. However, it *is* important to find the right balance between personalization and disjointed messaging. Your sales team has to hit the big beats of whatever you're marketing. It's your job as marketers to make sure they do.

In chapter 8, we joked about the Google trap. If your sales team is struggling to find the right marketing assets, they turn to Google as their logical-yet-illogical resource. They may find something related to what they're looking for, but because Google's indexing process takes a while, it may not be relevant anymore or align to that particular stage of the buyer journey.

If you don't commit to organizing your content and making it searchable under parameters such as topic, persona, stage of the buyer's journey, etc., you're not going to solve this problem. Google can't offer your sales team this kind of organization. You can. By controlling this process, you empower your sales reps by providing them with the right content at the right time. From there, they're free to customize their approach the rest of the way.

When we discovered that each of the sales reps at Uberflip were operating with their own slide decks, narratives, and go-to content assets, we knew we needed to change the way we did things. We doubled down on our own efforts to apply the Content Experience Framework to our organization. First, we centralized the right assets for them to use and then provided a tagging structure for them to find what they were looking for by stage. Then, rather than forcing them all to use one deck for every lead, we organized our slides so that they could be personalized along different industries, stages of the buyer journey, goals, and outcomes. Our reps still had to use our slides, but they could combine and leverage them however they needed to tell the story they were looking for.

PRE-SALE JOURNEY

Awareness	Consideration	Decision	Customer
Ebook	Webinars	Case Studies	Contract
Educational Content	Expert Guides	Product Sheets	Billing Invoices
Reports	Podcasts	Vendor Comparisons	Kickoff Survey
Influencer Content	Product Videos	Product Demo	Welcome Package

Search Engines | Live Chat | Social | Email
Paid Ads | Events | Phone | Partnerships

POST-SALE CONTENT EXPERIENCE

The same need to create a unified content experience holds true for post-sale or customer success. Every one of your customers may use your solution in a unique way. Your goal at the end of the day is to turn your customer into an advocate. If the customer doesn't know what your company stands for or if your company messaging is not aligned at every stage, you risk your customer advocates going out and describing your solution in a way that differs from what you may want.

Of course, this is the *best* worst problem. Imagine people who love your solution, but each describe your solution in a unique way. Many sectors have their own review sites their customers like to turn to so they can learn more about a particular product or offering. If you're in vacation rentals, it's sites like TripAdvisor. If you're in tech, it's sites like G2 Crowd and TrustRadius. On sites like these, past customers and advocates have a lot of sway over whether prospects will buy from you or simply why they inquire. If their messaging is disjointed, it means your messaging to them was disjointed, too.

Like I said, this is a *good* bad outcome. A *bad* bad outcome is where a customer is not armed with the right content to understand the value of your offering and fully adopt all its features and functionality. In those cases, you risk losing a customer to another company who figured out how to articulate their value and fully own their content experience throughout the post-sale experience.

Take it a step further and think about the impact content experience can have on product adoption. If your sales team sold your product and its features one way but your success team's training decks frame it in another way, this can cause distrust in your business—or worse, cause confusion and lack of adoption. This may feel like a stretch for some, but I can say from experience that if I don't understand the benefits of each feature in relation to the problems I bought the product to solve (i.e., the magic beans that aren't so magical), that's when I move into the dreaded "at risk for churn" territory. Having a consistent content experience from pre- to post-sale will ensure your customers onboard and adopt the product without any hesitation or confusion.

To illustrate, many post-sale organizations have technical writers who create knowledge-based content that may be disjointed from your original messaging that marketing is trying to align throughout your business. They may be providing helpful content with onboarding, frequently asked questions, and how-tos, but if it represents a tonal shift from your pre-sale content, then it will create a bit of cognitive dissonance among your customers.

Here's a list of some of the forms of content that pulse through a post-sale organization:

POST-SALE JOURNEY

Onboarding	Retention/ Advocacy	Churn	Winback
Knowledge Base	Core Lifecycle Nurture	Transactional Emails	Exit Survey
Onboarding Nurture	Newsletter	NPS Survey	Product Updates
Product Tour	Advocacy Content	Re-Engagement Nurture	Pricing Updates
Training Decks	Referral Content		Educational Content

Platform | Website | Live Chat | Phone | Social
Email | Resources | Knowledge Base | Events

SO, WHO THE F#CK IS IN CHARGE?

Usually, in Part III of a book, you start to feel resolve. After reading this chapter, you might feel more overwhelmed than ever. "Who the f#ck is in charge of all this?" you might say, and you'd be right to ask.

With so many content assets in an organization, it can be tough figuring out who owns what and when. On the post-sale side of things, for instance, who do you give this responsibility to? As we just explored: it could be a post-sale operations manager, a sales enablement manager, or even the VP of success. It's scary to think there's so many people who may be trying to help but may be doing damage instead.

Everyone in your organization is responsible for the content experience because everyone in your organization creates and uses content. Within each department, you will need to establish a key role or point person to ensure that messaging is consistent throughout the entire journey. However, that alone won't guarantee that what happens in sales is going to align with what happens in success, billing, and so on. As we'll discuss next chapter, the responsibility of creating a seamless content experience falls on the marketing team.

CHAPTER 12

THE MARKETING TEAM

———

Sorry for the second hockey analogy to follow (shouldn't be surprising, given I am Canadian). In hockey, as in any sport, there is no shortage of examples of teams looking good on paper, but just not coming together. Whenever that happens, a common refrain usually erupts from the fan base: fire the coach.[23]

You ever wonder why that is? You rarely hear calls for a team to a fire a player, and you practically never hear anyone demanding that a whole team be replaced. Nope, the coach is always the one to take the fall. It's not always fair—but that's just how things go.

Now, I like to think of myself as a pretty compassionate

---

23   Even as a volunteer coach for my kids' hockey teams, I've feared being replaced. No hockey fans are harsher critics than the parents of the players.

guy. Whenever problems arise, I always try to look past the person getting all the blame pinned on them to the root cause of the problem. As much as a coach is responsible for getting their team on the right path and creating leadership, there's only so much a coach can do with the team they're given. The coach may bring the team together, in other words, but you still need a good goalie, good forwards, and good defense.

Similarly, your content marketers could be doing their job perfectly, setting your team up for shot after shot (with asset after asset). However, if you don't have anyone in place to take those shots, then it's all for nothing. Is it the content marketer's fault if their content doesn't generate the ROI that everyone was hoping for? Of course not, if it's sitting unused.

Way back in the introduction, we talked about the kinds of professional training and experience that content marketers usually have coming into an organization. A large percentage are trained as journalists and writers before they become content marketers. Their expertise is in creating strong, narrative-driven content to attract the attention of their audience. Again, that's a full-time job all on its own. When we ask them to play all the other positions of our Content Experience Framework—centralize, organize, personalize, distribute, and generate results—we're simply asking too much of them. Again, imagine asking your defenseman to score goals or your goal scorer to clear the puck. No content marketer, or even a team of content marketers, should own all these phases on their own.

As we stressed last chapter, the content experience is a team effort. If you're committed to creating a content experience that actually works, it's time to ask yourself: do you want your content marketers to be amazing writers and storytellers, or do you want them to become demand generation or digital marketing managers? In this, our final chapter, you're going to learn how to align your marketing team role by role so that everyone has a stake in creating a complete, end-to-end content experience.

THE CONTENT MARKETER

Sometimes, just like the head coach, it's the content marketers that are wrongfully getting the axe if their team isn't generating the wins that are expected of them. That's not fair. So, in order to avoid making scapegoats of these vital players, let's be crystal clear about the content marketer's primary responsibilities:

- Building and managing a rich editorial calendar of content that attracts a qualified audience.
- Creating content such as blog posts, white papers, ebooks, reports, webinars, and infographics for the buyer journey.

- Taking stock of the content that exists for the organization to reference and leverage in the experiences to be built and campaigns to be run.
- Measuring and reporting on the effectiveness of the content they create.

Ultimately, our expectation is that the content marketer will generate content that creates new leads by converting site traffic through CTAs, landing pages, and gated content. It's not that the content marketer doesn't care about the experience—or that we shouldn't expect them to contribute—but rather, that they can only do so much on their own. When you have an entire marketing team aligned around the content experience, it's that much easier for the individual players to do their part.

As we've unpacked this book, we've explored a series of strategies (even an entire framework!) focused on the idea of personalizing the experience and organizing and distributing content in a way that leads customers from one asset to the next. These are important strategies, of course, but they're not exactly tied to the content marketer's responsibilities. In a large organization, you probably don't want the person creating the content to map the journeys. As we'll discuss just a little bit later, managing the content experience should be a separate role.

In terms of content experience, the content marketer is focused primarily on the first two phases of our framework—centralizing and organizing—though sometimes on personalizing as well. Their biggest concern in this role is making sure the content is subjectively organized by properly tagging it. This makes all new content easily discoverable for the rest of the team, allowing them to take those assets and build out personalized experiences. They're a contributor to the content experience, in other words, but they're not responsible for the end-to-end experience.

It's only natural for the content marketer to care about the content experience in that experience will impact engagement in the content they've created. They want their content to be easily found, leveraged, and consumed because they're just as interested in their conversions and meeting their KPIs as anyone else on the marketing team. But again, it's important to remember they are just a *part* of a team—and the best teams have clearly defined roles. Content marketers contribute best to the content experience when they're focused on being the secret sauce of the content experience, on being the expert storytellers who help drive engagement—and thereby drive conversion, generate leads, and retain customers. When they aren't stuck worrying about user paths, coding, or building out the visual components of a site, they thrive.

THE DIGITAL MARKETER

Note that I've bucketed this one less as the digital marketer and more so as a group of marketers focused on digital marketing. There's no shortage of people who contribute to digital marketing in one way or another. In fact, of my 7,169 LinkedIn connections at the time of writing this book, 3,533 are recommended when I search for "digital marketing." My goal is not to define digital marketing: I'm working hard enough to redefine content marketing here! So for the purposes of this section, let's just say that digital marketers can include people with this title, but also roles tied to but not limited to web, paid, social media, SEO, SEM, and even email. For their role in creating a complete content experience, digital marketers are focused on planning and executing on all digital marketing. Their duties include:

- Measuring and reporting the performance of all digital marketing campaigns and assessing that performance in relation to marketing goals.
- Collaborating with internal teams to create landing pages and optimize user experiences by utilizing strong analytical abilities to evaluate intent and customer experiences across multiple channels and customer touchpoints.
- Identifying and evaluating emerging technologies for potential addition to the marketing technology stack.

Keeping in mind these responsibilities, it becomes easy to see how digital marketers are responsible for optimizing the user experience. They're the ones you can count on to ensure you're on track. Their job is to find efficiencies within user agreement paths and leverage the right tools to optimize them further. Naturally, a key element connected to these user paths is content, so the digital marketer becomes instrumental in personalizing the content experience so they can arm the demand generation team with assets for their campaigns.

THE GRAPHIC AND UX DESIGNER

Some digital marketers can design beautiful things, but finding a digital marketer with those tools (sans a tool like Canva) is a little like finding a unicorn. Most organizations need to rely on graphic designers and user experience (UX) designers—who I'm going to group together for the purposes of getting you to the end of this book—when considering the visual components of their content. Both graphic and UX designers are often focused on:

- Translating concepts into user flows, wireframes, and mockups that lead to intuitive user experiences.
- Rapidly testing and iterating based on a user-centered design approach.
- Designing and delivering wireframes, user stories,

and user journeys optimized for a wide range of devices and interfaces.

At the end of the day, members of these groups are responsible for creating and maintaining the visual representation of the brand or company. As marketers, we know that the visual design and aesthetic of our assets can massively impact engagement and conversion. And, since a key part of the content experience is focusing on the *environment*, your design teams are crucial to making sure your brand is represented correctly.

Your graphic and UX teams are tasked with making sure your content assets are easy to find, intuitive, and make sense to the end user, while at the same time making sure that all visual components are executed consistently—from your main website to other indicators of your brand identity. In terms of the Content Experience Framework, then, these team members are heavily involved in the personalization and distribution phases, working to ensure that all content assets, from creative templates to email, are aligned within your brand.

THE DEMAND GENERATION MARKETER

As the players most focused on getting more qualified leads and sales, demand generation marketers are often set up to take home the award (or failure) for outcomes, fair or not. Demand generation marketers can sometimes be the content marketer's toughest critic because they can blame a crappy asset for not creating demand for a business or product. In truth, however, they often impact content performance just as much as the content marketer. At any rate, having your demand generation marketers at the table is important in order to help the rest of the team decide which products are mapped to which user experiences.

The demand generation marketer relies heavily on measurement and attribution of their content assets, and they use that data to choose the right channels to engage prospective customers to accelerate pipeline velocity. Since demand generation marketers often control a huge chunk of the budget, they have a tremendous impact on the distribution phase of our Content Experience Framework. However, given the rise of one-to-one marketing, what they often don't realize is that they have a considerable stake in the personalization phase as well.

Too often, organizations assume that the demand generation marketer will simply distribute. They think more about the cadence and the dollars and less about the ingredients that go into tactics, which are heavily made up of content. If they're only focused on distribution and aren't aware of that personalization process, they won't know how to effectively map their content to the buyer journey.

Take, for example, delivering a retargeting ad on Google. Many marketers judge purely based on whether Google was effective as an ad platform, rather than on whether the ad itself was compelling or if the person who clicked on the ad landed into an immersive experience. To get this right, demand generation marketers and content marketers need to work together if either is to own their part of the content experience. To succeed, the demand generation marketer absolutely needs good content and resources to optimize the conversion path that they put before their audience.

To recap, the demand generation marketer is focused on:

- Getting more marketing-qualified leads to sales.
- Measurement and attribution.
- Analyzing and interpreting data points across paid marketing efforts and providing feedback to continually enhance performance.
- Ensuring reporting is correct and complete on an ongoing basis.

To wrap the complicated debate over who owns the content experience, the following table illustrates how content experience impacts each role we've discussed.

CONTENT EXPERIENCE OWNERSHIP

ROLE	Centralize Content	Organize Content	Personalize Experiences	Distribute Content	Generate Results
Content Marketer Content creation and management	●	●	●		●
Demand Generation Marketer Generate pipeline and revenue			●	●	●
Digital Marketer Campaign and website performance/ User experience		●	●	●	●
UX Designer/ Graphic Designer User experience/ Visual aesthetics		●	●		●

INTRODUCING THE CONTENT EXPERIENCE MANAGER

Right about now, you're remembering that thought you had at the end of the last chapter. "Who's responsible for all of this, Randy?" you asked, and I promised I would answer that question here. So let's get to it.

Each of the marketing roles outlined so far in this chapter is invested in the content experience, but each in a different way. Players at any one of these positions could (and do) own a slice of the content experience pie. However, no one position can (or should) own the content experience in its entirely. If this is what your marketing organization looks like, you've essentially got a team of potential all-stars, but no coach to guide them.

Enter the content experience manager.

Suggesting a new role is always pretty bold—how do we know when it's time? Well, let me take you back in time. At an Uberflip company-wide fiscal kickoff, our CEO invited two of the co-founders of Eloqua, Paul Tashima and Steve Woods, to walk us through the rise of marketing automation as a category. Eloqua, a marketing automation platform later acquired by Oracle for $871 million after going public, very much defined the category of marketing automation.

During a Q&A, one of our team members asked Steve a question: *"Who were you selling to in the early days?"*

Steve chuckled and began describing a marketer who was overly focused on data and acted more like an analyst than the creative rock star people had historically built around. Remember, this was back in the early 2000s, and at the time, marketers like these were routinely defined as just *weird*! This time everyone on our team chuckled—even the demand generation team, which he was describing an early version of. These *weird* marketers were demand generation, marketing operations, and account-based marketers before they existed. What was considered weird at that point was now the norm and a role we couldn't imagine living without. And now, fifteen years later, we welcome another *weird marketer* to the fold.

A skilled content experience manager is capable not only of unifying your marketing team, but also of interfacing with the rest of your organization and making sure your content experience is aligned across departments (just like we discussed in the last chapter!) If you're looking for a good comparison of what a content experience manager does, the sales enablement manager might come closest, as each is deeply concerned with how content is presented to prospects and customers as a reflection of the business. A stat from Salesforce says 50 percent of deals stall in a pipeline due to the customer not understanding the relevance of the product or service. The sales enablement manager is tasked with ensuring sales reps place content in ways that create an experience by considering the greater environment, ensuring proper structure, and assessing their ability to increase engagement. The problem for sales enablement managers, however, is that they have no one to provide feedback or facilitate requests to the marketing team. With no checks and nobody minding the big picture, breakdowns begin to happen—such as the content marketer getting continual requests to create new content when similar assets might already exist.

That's why having a content experience manager is so important. Some organizations are already hiring for this or similar roles. While the precise descriptions and responsibilities vary, common elements include:

- Being able to identify the right assets for the right place in the funnel to arm sales with personalized content experiences.
- Facilitating communication between the demand generation team and the content marketing team to ensure their goals are clearly communicated between the earliest and latest steps of the Content Experience Framework.
- Acting as liaison between departments to ensure organizational alignment of the content experience between departments.

In our experience at Uberflip, having a content experience manager (or in our case, a director of content experience) has been invaluable. In the months leading up to us creating a dedicated role, I began to detect a lack of communication and collaboration between individual pieces of the organization. This is not to take away from the people on our team. They all were wonderful individuals doing great work, but they weren't working toward a unified content strategy. When I looked into trying to solve the issue, I looked to other companies to see what we could learn.

What I learned was that, while many organizations had been proactive by placing people in roles like "director of content," those roles often came with considerable ambiguity. For the roles that *were* more clearly defined, you could just as easily have called them "director of writing strategy," as their responsibilities usually ended there.

I realized that no one had entirely solved this puzzle, but I knew there were still lessons to be had, so I asked as many questions as I could. Who were they writing for? What type of tone do they have? What did their editorial calendar look like? Outside of the rare superstar directors of content, most admittedly were not collaborating on the editorial calendar based on the needs of the demand generation team. Often, they were too focused on the content and writing, and not enough on understanding the journey.

I didn't just want someone who could own the content. And I didn't want us only talking about content experience as a team without buying into creating great content experiences as a goal. What I wanted was someone who could *own* the content experience from end to end. So, we brought in someone with seniority who could work proactively among the many different personalities both on our marketing team and across the organization.

While the exact role of the content experience manager

will vary from organization to organization, here's how we define it:

> The Content Experience Manager is responsible for managing and optimizing the end-to-end, omnichannel experiences around content, including but not limited to blogs, resources, white papers, ebooks, videos, podcasts, webinars, customer and prospect emails, sales collateral, and online properties. This position reports to the VP of Marketing (or CMO) and works cross-functionally and collaboratively within the marketing department and across the entire organization.

For a more detailed overview of roles and responsibilities for this individual, see the appendix of the book. This should give you a good jumpstart when you sit down to write your own job description.

OWN THE CONTENT EXPERIENCE

When you align your marketing team around the content experience—and when you have a dedicated content experience manager to own that experience—you bring validity, accountability, and visibility to your content marketing (creation) efforts. To do that, however, both the content experience manager and the marketing team in general need to be ready to champion their responsibilities and own their role in the Content Experience Framework.

At Uberflip, when we introduced the idea of the director of content experience and restructured some of our content team to align with our goals, we saw some resistance at first. Some on the marketing team questioned whether it would have been better to hire a writer focused on brand identity. However, such a hire would have just perpetuated the same problem that led to this book in the first place. Assigning roles and liaising between departments isn't a writer's job. Writing good content is.

We knew we needed someone who could provide the depth of knowledge and thought leadership to ensure our content experience ran smoothly from end to end—and more importantly, that their efforts would directly correlate with positive revenue. So, we took the plunge, went all-in on content experience, and never looked back.

CHAPTER 13

COMMITTING TO CONTENT EXPERIENCE

———

Over the years, as our company grew its content, we were always trying to use different images, frameworks, and guides to help people understand the value our organization could add. Well before the Content Experience Framework existed, there was an image we all liked that we felt best summed up the value we added to other organizations. We called it the ConEx Wheel. Don't worry: this isn't another "bonus" framework, but rather a story of what happens when your organization is not aligned!

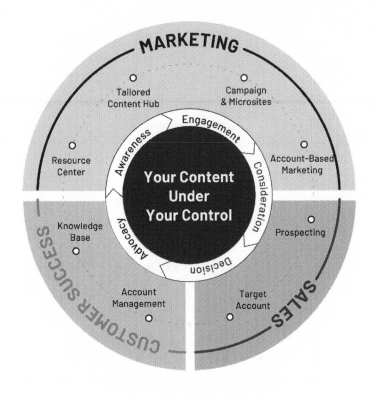

THE CONEX WHEEL

In this image, you can see the different people in an organization who touch different types of content at different stages of the buyer journey. The idea was simple: each needs this content at their fingertips to do their job effectively. One look at this image, and you'll see that it aligns closely with the topics we've just hit in this book.

Unfortunately, the very creation and dissemination of this image also led to a realization: we weren't owning the content experience as we should have been. How did this image teach us that? All you sci-fi fans are going to love this story.

As we distributed the image from department to department, each adapted it to their own purposes and began to use it and refer to it in different ways. The people in customer success called it by its proper name, the ConEx Wheel, while others referred to it as the "Content Experience Journey." It even took form as a boat steering wheel (which I'll take blame for) nicknamed "The Helm." Over in sales, they had a name for it that had me reeling back in horror: "The Death Star."

Full disclosure, I'm one of the five people on the planet who is not a Star Wars fan. I don't know much about it. However, I *do* know that the Death Star was the evil killing machine that was not Jedi-friendly. Hearing our ConEx Wheel referred to as an evil killing machine made me realize that we had major, major brand identity issues. I resolved to understand why.

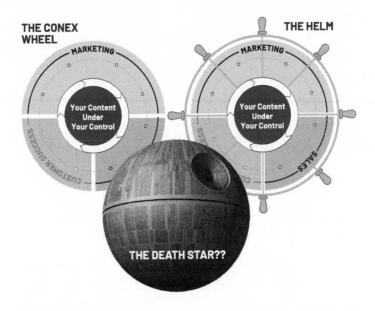

THE CONEX WHEEL

THE HELM

THE DEATH STAR??

For the next few weeks, I spoke with different team members in different departments. I asked them how they wrote about the content experience in general and the ConEx Wheel in particular. Everybody had a different answer. Some mostly had it right, but there were inconsistencies to their approach and messaging. Others were spinning up content and narratives that simply didn't fit within the experience we were trying to drive our customer through. If someone sees both the Death Star and the ConEx Wheel and doesn't understand that they're one and the same—let alone that one is an evil killing machine and the other is a helpful framework—that's a dysfunction of the highest order.

An image alone doesn't make or break content experience, but this was the beginning of broken messaging—or as we called it earlier, broken telephone syndrome. As I outlined in the previous chapter, imagine if, pre-sale, our prospects saw the Death Star (thanks, sales). Then, as they were being onboarded post-sale, they saw a similar wheel that took on a different name, but for all intents and purposes was the exact same thing (cue success rep). Then, icing on the cake, the CMO calls it a f#ckin' *Helm*! Don't you think, as a customer, this would be a very confusing experience? The problem here was no one was owning the journey. We had other assets supporting each image—so it was no surprise that content wasn't being used and no surprise no one referred to our Wheel/Helm/Death Star in online reviews.

It was clear we didn't have a cohesive content experience. But that said, it also wasn't outside of our reach. Seeing the problem, we resolved to invest in our team, player by player. Our mission was to secure buy-in to the idea that taking a customer on a unified journey requires not just one person, but an entire organization. It took some work, but today I'm happy to report that it's been a long time since I've heard anything in our organization being referred to as a killing machine.

WHO BENEFITS MOST?

While the Content Experience Framework was still in

draft mode, I was in a meeting with Laura Ramos from Forrester. I walked her through the need to *centralize* content, *organize* with care, *personalize* the experience, and *distribute* in campaigns, all in order to *generate results*. I asked her for feedback on whether this framework might help fuel demand and revenue. She liked it, saying that a lot of what was addressed in our (proposed) framework aligned with her concepts of creating more customer engagement. Then, she shared her version of the content experience, a series of perfectly choreographed dance steps we lead the buyer through before they're ready to buy.

She challenged me with a question: who in my organization would benefit most from our Content Experience Framework?

The question caught me off guard. My initial gut response was the marketing team. In theory, this framework would empower our team to create great marketing campaigns that were truly personalized—and to do it at scale. Often, I lead round tables with marketers where they talk about that one campaign they did that they knocked out of the park or the big account they landed. Rarely were they able to take that win and scale it for their business in a game-changing way. With this framework, I was certain we'd found the key—even for ourselves.

Remember the story of Snowflake's Daniel Day from chapter 8? The first thing Daniel did was hire great people and adopt a process. He did it for a dozen accounts on a sparse budget and proved that his model worked. After achieving this proof of concept, his team adopted the Content Experience Framework, powered by a CEP to help him scale. Today, Snowflake is still killing it—thanks to a well-balanced combination of people, process, and technology—personalizing engagement for over three hundred unique accounts every quarter last I spoke to Daniel.

After I finished sharing my initial thoughts with Laura, she said, "That was a good answer, but there's someone even more impacted by this model." She then pointed to the success and account management teams that apply this framework one-on-one with their customers, the people for whom it is crucial they buy into this model if they want to see success. The best ones, she said, tell a consistent story that aligns with your organization and creates a ripple effect with future buyers through advocacy.

She was right. Ultimately, if you can't secure organization buy-in for the Content Experience Framework, or really any other initiative you can think of, it's not just the individual departments that end up playing broken telephone. It's every prospective customer considering working with your organization. It was then I realized this book would not just stop at driving demand and revenue, but also relationships.

IT'S ALL ABOUT LIFETIME VALUE

We live in a day and age of high turnover for marketers in our organizations. For this reason, many of us need to think about not just the lifetime value of a customer, but the lifetime value of a contact (or champion). A contact may go on to another company and buy from you again. It is important that they maintain an understanding of what your company stands for so they can be your champion wherever they land next.

Furthermore, with the rise of user review sites such as G2 Crowd for tech software, TripAdvisor for hotels, and many other niche sites tied to different industries, we have to deal with not just bad, but good reviews that might position us in ways we may not want. If we have a consistent content experience, we ensure that we maintain a consistent brand identity and our advocates line up an ongoing cycle of advocacy and referrals. This, in theory, means future net new, and expansion revenue opportunities. In order for it to work, though, everyone needs to be bought in so that pre- and post-sale departments provide the same consistent experiences.

As you near the end of this book, you're probably wondering, *What do I do next? Do I need to build a Spotify engine that can deliver Made For You experiences? Do I need to hire a content experience manager?*

What *do* you do next?

Here's my challenge to you. I want you to go to your boss or the person setting direction for the company message and journey. This may be the CEO or the CMO. (I bet you know the person who's ignoring the experience in your organization.) You're going to need to prep yourself with two things before you enter this person's office:

- *Step 1*: Down a Red Bull, do ten pushups, or listen to "Thunderstruck" by AC/DC on Spotify—whatever gets you going.
- *Step 2*: Because not everyone is as comfortable dropping an F-bomb as I am, grab a copy of this book as your scapegoat.

Now with all that energy from Step 1, I want you to strut in with confidence (but not cockiness—no one likes that) and say the following: "We're wasting dollars, we're wasting time, we're wasting our content, we're wasting our opportunity. If we're going to win—f#ck content marketing—let's focus on content experience!" At this time, on cue, feel free to slam down the book on the desk (without breaking any glass desks). It's all about emphasis.

Now remember, the person you brought the thunder to didn't see this coming. They likely aren't losing sleep over content. The truth is, they probably don't realize that every way you go to market, whether you're invested in inbound, demand generation, account-based marketing, or sales enablement, the road to success is paved in content. For every campaign, every strategy, every word that comes out of a sales rep's mouth, it all begins with content. So don't lose faith if they look at you like a *weird* marketer. This is where you can tell them that Eloqua story of early demand generation marketers being *weird,* or better yet, tell them to read the book and that you'll be back on Monday ready to break down your content experience with them.

As you walk out of the room after this dramatic moment, you will have initiated change—and that will feel weird at first. Committing to the content experience isn't about getting permission to create more, higher-quality content—*you will be challenged here, of course*. It's about injecting the right content in front of the right people at the right time no matter how we go to market. If your organization can buy in to this framework, then you will have put your company on a much more aggressive growth path.

Just remember, if your organization *does* choose to commit to the Content Experience Framework, make sure you do it right. Find a content experience manager who can rally everyone behind the idea and align the organization around your cause. Follow through with every step of the framework. Audit your own work constantly—and know that there's always room for improvement.

The biggest goal for an organization is growth. The content experience is your secret weapon for driving demand, revenue, and relationships.

So, for the last time, let's practice together. Say it with me now out loud:

F#ck content marketing.

Focus on content experience.

AFTERWORD

A LOOK TO THE FUTURE
WITH YOAV SCHWARTZ

———

Welcome, reader, to the Afterword. I'm your host, Yoav Schwartz. According to Kindle statistics, only a relatively small percentage of readers make it to the end of a book. That means, if you're reading this, you're part of an exclusive club. And to honor that, I'd like to give you a prize: more content!

Let's start with an observation from a very wise person who is near and dear to my heart:

> We're at an interesting time where in modern organizations, the CMO (people like Randy) is gaining budget over the CIO—scary but true. Here's my rhetorical question to you: What do you expect them to do with that budget? Keep

investing in technologies that the CIO wants to deploy, or invest in technologies that help that CMO and their team?

All throughout this book, Randy hit on the idea of investing first in people, then in process, and finally in technology. Now that we know that CMOs are gaining more budget year-over-year—the question is, what form of technology is best going to arm the content experience manager in the future?

As budget continues to flow from the CIO over to the CMO—and as we continue to see the need to personalize at scale—some new buyers have rolled into town: the content experience manager, the demand generation marketer, and the digital marketing team. They are the ones who need to centralize, organize, personalize, distribute, and generate results in order to help your organization create a seamless content experience. And to do that, they're going to need the right tools for the job. Traditionally, that's been the content management system (CMS). However, for reasons I will explain, the days of the CMS are numbered.

THE INNOVATOR'S DILEMMA

In the book *The Innovator's Dilemma*, author Clayton M. Christensen argues that it doesn't matter how innovative you are. Eventually you will fall into an innovation trap:

1. Your innovation brings you success.
2. Your success earns you a bunch of customers.
3. Your customers want you to keep doing what's important to them.

For a while, this is a pretty good deal. However, eventually it leads to problems. By focusing only on your customers and what they want, eventually you drop the ball, ignoring a new, rising market that will inevitably disrupt your business. Personally, I believe if you're not going to disrupt yourself, someone else will.

To illustrate how this process works, let's take a look at BlackBerry, the once proud titan of the mobile phone industry. Back before Apple introduced the iPhone, BlackBerry was happily chugging along and growing at an incredible rate. By selling to the IT teams of an organization, BlackBerry had found a recipe for seemingly unlimited success.

Naturally, since members of the IT teams were their primary customer, BlackBerry leaned on them for future product development. If the IT team wanted more security, BlackBerry gave them more security. If they wanted a better keyboard or improved email functionality, BlackBerry was all too happy to oblige.

Suddenly, in comes a new buyer group—the consumer—

and they had wildly different demands. "I don't give a sh#t about a keyboard," they said. "I just want better apps, a bigger screen, and all these other fun features for my day-to-day."

Unfortunately for consumers, BlackBerry wasn't listening. After all, their buyers were the IT crowd. Why should they care about what consumers wanted?

In comes the iPhone with a simple message for consumers: we're listening. Because the IT crowd was still the primary market for smartphone buyers, the iPhone didn't dominate on day one. Apple continued to grow the consumer market for smartphones, and then, by building in the minimum requirements necessary to appease the IT teams, soon they'd made inroads on that market too.

Meanwhile, BlackBerry still wasn't listening to the consumer—and soon, it became obvious that they were no longer listening to the IT team either, whose priorities had shifted with the rise of a different option. If you were to draw this out in a line graph, you'd see consumers overtake the IT department in terms of influence on the market.

When BlackBerry first hit the market, they disrupted the entire cellular phone industry, pushing the limits of what was thought possible with a handheld device. They were the innovators. However, when it came time to expand their business, they narrowed their market to government and large enterprise contractors. These customers didn't care about games, chat, and full-screen browsing. They cared about security and having a good keyboard. BlackBerry was so laser-focused on this market that they ignored a potentially larger and more lucrative market: the everyday consumer. As a result, they dropped the ball and were overtaken by Apple.

THE CMS PROBLEM

From our perspective, the same thing that happened to BlackBerry is currently happening to the CMS. The CMS started off as a great solution to a new problem. As soon as the internet demonstrated itself to be a viable marketing opportunity, companies everywhere started scrambling to get their content online.

Quickly, CMS platforms like WordPress and Drupal rose up to fill that need. They said, "Here's a way to manage a bunch of different pages of content at once," and all the companies flocked to them. For nearly two decades, the CMS has been the go-to platform for hosting and managing content, housing websites, blogs, and sites where the boundaries between the two aren't especially clear. In a simpler time, the CMS was great at managing these assets. However, today, it's being used to power extremely complicated web experiences filled with various forms of content. To put it bluntly, everything that a marketer needs to do today is nothing that the CMS was built for.

This has left marketers with two options. The first is to cling desperately to a sinking ship, maximizing those CMSs for everything they're worth through a strange alchemy of customization, hackery, and plug-ins, and hoping that's enough. The problem is, in this scenario, marketers don't own the experiences they're trying to build, because they're at the whims of whatever their IT team was able to cobble together using a technology solution that was never intended for marketing. As Randy outlined using the Content Experience Framework in this book, the marketer must be in control of the infrastructure in order to be able to create content experiences at scale.

Many organizations are limping along with these cobbled-together solutions, but there will come a time soon when the bottom falls out. Why? Because today's marketers don't simply need to create these great destinations; they need to be able to change those destinations day in and day out. To do that, they need tools that are designed for *them*—not for IT, not for an agency, and not for software developers.

This brings us to our second option: the practitioner-led platform. If you look at the pattern of tech development over the past couple decades, the market is headed there already. While do-it-all platforms like WordPress, Drupal, and Magento were built for developers, subsequent platforms have challenged the incumbent by offering an experience built around the needs of a particular function. For instance, Shopify is built around the needs of a store owner, and Wix and Squarespace are built around the needs of the business owner. This, of course, begs the question: where is the practitioner-led platform for marketers?

Enter the content experience platform (CEP). The companies building CEPs recognize that marketers have the entire buyer journey to worry about—not just top-of-the-funnel and search engine optimized experiences, but also demand generation, sales enablement, and potentially even richer experiences for customer success. A CMS is not designed for that scale of content, nor is it designed for the end user. The CEP is.

As I see it, there are two primary advantages to a CEP.

ADVANTAGE #1: SCALABLE MULTIFORMAT CONTENT MANAGEMENT

A CMS can only provide one format: the webpage. Sure, you can plug whatever content you'd like into that page, but at the end of the day, that's your only option. A CEP, on the other hand, treats every content type as a different entity. A blog post is still a blog post, but if you're starting from a different asset—a video, for instance—the CEP treats it as the core piece of content, not an embed. For every type of asset you can think of, whether a slide deck, a white paper, or a social post, the CEP manages it independently of a typical page structure.

ADVANTAGE #2: DEEP INTEGRATION INTO OTHER MARKETING TECHNOLOGIES

The concept of demand generation is tightly integrated into a modern marketer's needs. Using it in parallel with a CMS is a very different story than using it when it's tightly integrated into a CEP. With a CEP, marketers no longer have to bang their head against the wall trying to figure out how to gate assets. The answer is integrated into a purpose-built solution designed for the buyer's journey. Again, this highlights that the CEP was designed for the *marketer*, not for IT.

For these reasons, I see it as an inevitability that the CEP will eventually overtake the CMS—and soon. At the end of the day, marketers are going to invest in marketing-friendly tech. The CMS has served marketers as well as it could over the past couple decades, but ultimately the marketer isn't their customer. And so, armed with a bigger slice of the budget pie than ever before, CMOs will simply start looking somewhere else to spend on tech.

HOW THE CEP WORKS

No CMS was designed to provide marketers with analytics. Some have built-in integrations for features like Google Analytics, but that only yields surface-level, SEO-related insights. And while those can be of some value to the marketer, when it comes to gaining insight across the different stages of the journey or regarding multi-touch attribution, forget about it. Because the CEP is tied deeply into your other systems, we can probe much deeper into understanding our customers. As a result, as Randy put it, personalization is no longer simply, "Hey Bob from Acme, here's a generic experience that's the same for everyone, but I added your name to the front of it."

Instead, it becomes, "Hey Bob, I know that you are 60 percent deep into your journey with us, and other companies in your industry at this point have found these four assets helpful." Here's where the AI engine kicks in. Using third-party data, your AI can recognize the visitor, determine where they are in the buying cycle, and create a robust, malleable content experience. It can de-prioritize out-of-date assets, make educated guesses on new assets that have received views from similar buyers, and so on until it has landed on the four best pieces of content to show Bob.

This added layer of presentation makes a world of difference when it comes to getting the buyer to self-discover and find the information they're looking for. This is great news for marketers in the B2B and considered purchase world, which is relentlessly focused on creating efficiency and shortening the buyer cycle (and then doing it all over again). While a CMS essentially provides a dead end for every campaign, the CEP helps marketers generate fresh insights and improve their execution at every stage of the buyer journey.

ABM is a great example of this process in action. ABM is a great approach, albeit one wholly dependent on personalization. Managing fifty accounts under ABM is one thing, but what about five thousand? If you want to avoid resorting to working off of personas, automating your personalization is your only option. Powered by a CEP, instead of feeling like one out of five thousand, your accounts will feel like they're one out of five—each of whom you spent a ton of time investigating and putting a great experience in front of. To do this, you need to get deep into the data, figure out what makes them tick, and package your content accordingly.

Here, a note on AI. AI is currently playing the role of assistant, not orchestrator. A marketer can do fifty of something, but they can't do five thousand of something. So, if they can get the fifty somethings right, they can confidently enlist the help of AI to scale the process. As much as we might like to be, we aren't quite to the point where we can say, "You know what? I need a thousand leads," and expect AI to figure it out for us. For now, AI is simply a manifestation of what we tell it to do. Marketers still need to get their hands dirty and, over time, work to create really smart machines.

IT ALL HAPPENS IN THE EXPERIENCE

As marketers, we send a lot of emails. It's easy to understand why. When we look at marketing automation, every email is typically tied to one asset. If you want somebody to read through the content, the old-school approach is to send them at least three emails. Of course, with an overcrowded inbox, not everyone will click on each email and discover each asset.

A CEP changes the game by allowing you to marry your email to an entry point, rather than to a piece of content. In this process, we like to joke that it almost becomes a game of how many emails do I *not* need to send, because if I can send a person on a journey and get them to consume the assets I want them to, I won't need to.

That's the power of the content experience platform, because it's so deeply married to a marketer's campaigns and activities. It's not just one end point, not just one destination. It is a closed loop, the lifeblood of your campaign. Whether you want your buyer to consume content or fill out a form, it all happens in the experience. All your emails, tweets, and ads are simply different ways to start your buyer on their journey. If you can get them to stick with you once they land—to do not just one thing, but all the things you want them to—that's real scalability.

After all, more action from the buyer means less activity by the marketers—and in turn, fewer emails, fewer tweets, and deeper insights into what makes that visitor or client tick. To me, that's the real unsung benefit of a great content experience: having all the data points you need to understand how to continuously become more efficient with your campaigns.

YOUR CHALLENGE

Now that we're just about done, I want to leave you with a challenge.

Let's say you have one account you need to close—just this one company. To close it, you have to really dive in and figure out what makes them tick. Let's say you have your entire company at your disposal, with everyone focused solely on landing this account. How certain are you that you could do it? Could you actually figure out what is required to get this one person to click on an email, to get them to consume the right content that is perfectly personalized to their needs?

Most likely, you're not entirely sure. That's okay. I've asked this question to a lot of marketers, and I've yet to have anyone respond with 100 percent certainty that they could land that account. The question is, if you can't be certain of how you would perform with only one account, how would you feel about having to do that for $X,000$?

We're far, far away from that kind of certainty, especially at scale. In some ways, we're only now starting to even answer the right questions. However, with improvements in people, process, and technology, we're getting there.

Content comes in a variety of formats. Content needs to be measured in all different ways. A content management system needs to tie in deeply with other marketing technology. Marketers can continue to jam their CMS full of plug-ins and integrations, but at the end of the day, a CMS simply isn't designed for marketers. A CEP is. And that makes a big difference.

Yoav is a repeat tech founder and investor with a unique combination of creative, technical, and analytical skills (and musical talent of course!). In 2012, he partnered with Frisch, identifying a major gap in the content marketing space, to start Uberflip as CEO.

APPENDIX

CONTENT EXPERIENCE MANAGER JOB DESCRIPTION

———

Have I convinced you that you need to hire a content experience manager yet? If so, I give you full permission to take this job description and post it online!

CONTENT EXPERIENCE MANAGER

The Content Experience Manager is responsible for managing and optimizing the end-to-end, omnichannel experience around content, including but not limited to blogs, resources, white papers, ebooks, videos, podcasts, webinars, customer and prospect emails, sales collateral, and online properties. This position reports to the VP of Marketing (or CMO) and works cross-functionally and collaboratively within the marketing department and across the organization.

ROLE AND RESPONSIBILITIES

- Standardize brand and messages across all content to ensure a cohesive, singular experience.
- Strategize, map, update, and deliver new and existing content, assets, and collateral to a well-defined buyer journey for each of the sales and marketing team's buyer personas, including customer advocates, champions, and verticals.
- Assess and optimize the digital customer journey to ensure best-in-class UX across channels and devices.
- Advocate for the importance of content experience across the organization.
- Ensure on-site personalization and segmentation is consistent with the goals of the demand gen team.
- Oversee delivery of all content and assets and ensure it is tailored to specific personas/verticals.
- Build out a variety of experiences and content collections to be discovered by prospects and used by sales and marketing to direct buyer paths.

EXPERIENCE

We're looking for a full-stack marketer who is inspired by presenting thought-provoking stories and shaping a company's narrative through a prospect's experience.

The ideal candidate should possess:

- Five to ten years of marketing experience.
- Experience working cross-functionally both within marketing and with sales and success teams.
- An understanding of the buyer journey and ability to provide thoughtful analysis, and optimize based on data.
- Experience with UX design and branding an asset.
- Ability to work collaboratively as well as independently.
- An eye for analysis and detail, as well as strong creative chops.

ACKNOWLEDGMENTS

Yoav Schwartz

There is nothing better than celebrating success (and failure) with a partner. Yoav and I have worked together since 2010, launching Uberflip in 2012. Plain and simple, I wouldn't be here with the life experiences or focus on experience without his partnership. I am eternally grateful.

Paige Gerber & Christine Otsuka

This book is filled with my stories, but many people can tell you I am the master of tangents; squirrel. It took the skill of these two amazing marketers to ensure this book had focus. Even more, many of the ideas tied to the Content Experience Framework and definition can be attributed to their hard work and perspective.

Quentin Zancanaro

They say don't judge a book by its cover, but f#ck
it, we all do. Quentin rocked my cover as he does
pretty much every experience that's ever tied
to my personal (b-rand) or Uberflip brand.

Jon Miller

I've always been a marketer, but I'm still learning as
a tech founder. Having the ear and time of those who
have succeeded makes my journey a bit easier. Jon
has always made the time for me, and writing the
foreword for this book takes that to the next level.

Uberflip Customers

I only felt comfortable sharing these ideas because
we have customers who have validated them. It
is their trailblazing mentality that has allowed
content experience to rise as a category and focus.

Our Team

One of our core values at Uberflip is to *Create Great
Experiences*. Through that pursuit, we have been
able to create a movement, and I am grateful to both
our current team and those who helped us to build
a business and create a better way over the years.

Early Believers
Before we took a $32 million round of funding, we got to $10 million in revenue on just under $1 million in external capital. That money came from a small group of "angels" who believed in Content Experience before it was a category. You know who you are—thank you.

Chas
Your voice rocks—thanks for coaching me!

Anyone Who's Attended Conex
The focus on content experience is a movement. Like this book, it's not just about using Uberflip, but also about buying into the importance of content experience. Every summer (in partnership with my good friend Jay Baer), we bring together marketers and thought leaders in Toronto to talk about creating a winning experience, not just content.

My Family
It's taken a lot of time in the office and on the road to gain the perspective I've been able to share. The opportunity to invest that time is because I have the love, support, and encouragement of my wife Jenny (who encourages me to do what I love) and my kids Ethan, Lyla, and Ryan. I'm proud that some of my favorite stories in this book stem from interactions with them.

WHO IS THE REAL RANDY FRISCH?

Randy Frisch's favorite game growing up was "Two Truths and a Lie." (Okay, actually that's a lie. It was Operation.) In that spirit, rather than bore you with a normal author bio, we thought we'd have some fun. Try to guess which of the following are true or a lie.

1. To get some social media love, Uberflip co-founders Randy Frisch and Yoav Schwartz once lip-synced and danced to Drake's "In My Feelings" as part of the #InMyFeelings Challenge, atop the CN Tower in Toronto, over one thousand feet above the ground.
2. Randy is a computer programming whiz.
3. Before introducing Uberflip's technology to marketers, Randy tried to sell it as a content solution for media publishers.

4. Most of Randy's keynote presentations include metaphors, quotes, and references to his three kids.
5. Randy would spend so much time talking thought leader Jay Baer's ear off about the content experience that Jay finally threw up his arms and told Randy to start a podcast.

To find out what's true and what's a lie, visit b-rand.com/story.

CONTENT EXPERIENCE FRAMEWORK CUT-OUTS

———

As we explored a *Focus on Content Experience* requires a team effort. In case you're not ready to hand off the entire book the next 3 pages are cut-outs of the framework to share with your peers.

Add a note on the back and make it personal!

Content Experience Framework

The Best Way to Create Personalized Content Experiences

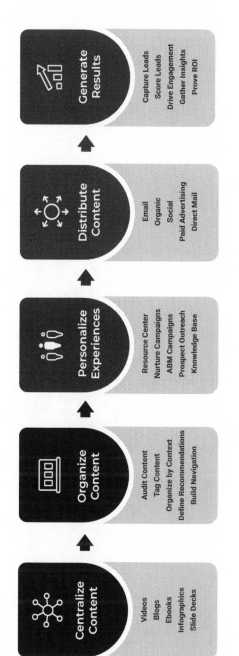

Centralize Content
- Videos
- Blogs
- Ebooks
- Infographics
- Slide Decks

Organize Content
- Audit Content
- Tag Content
- Organize by Context
- Define Recommendations
- Build Navigation

Personalize Experiences
- Resource Center
- Nurture Campaigns
- ABM Campaigns
- Prospect Outreach
- Knowledge Base

Distribute Content
- Email
- Organic
- Social
- Paid Advertising
- Direct Mail

Generate Results
- Capture Leads
- Score Leads
- Drive Engagement
- Gather Insights
- Prove ROI

Presented By Überflip

TO:

FROM:

LET'S FOCUS ON CONTENT EXPERIENCE

Content Experience Framework

The Best Way to Create Personalized Content Experiences

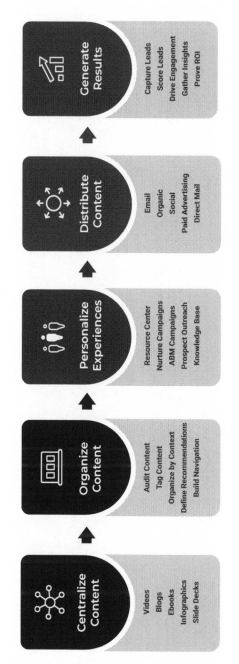

Centralize Content
- Videos
- Blogs
- Ebooks
- Infographics
- Slide Decks

Organize Content
- Audit Content
- Tag Content
- Organize by Context
- Define Recommendations
- Build Navigation

Personalize Experiences
- Resource Center
- Nurture Campaigns
- ABM Campaigns
- Prospect Outreach
- Knowledge Base

Distribute Content
- Email
- Organic
- Social
- Paid Advertising
- Direct Mail

Generate Results
- Capture Leads
- Score Leads
- Drive Engagement
- Gather Insights
- Prove ROI

Presented By Überflip

TO:

FROM:

LET'S FOCUS ON CONTENT EXPERIENCE

Content Experience Framework

The Best Way to Create Personalized Content Experiences

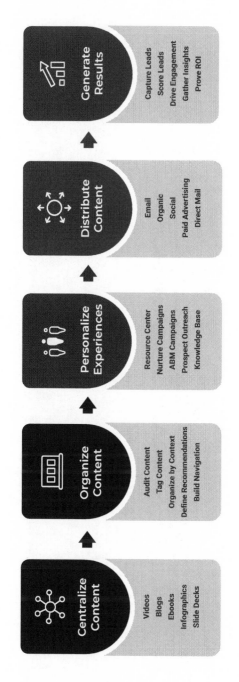

Centralize Content	Organize Content	Personalize Experiences	Distribute Content	Generate Results
Videos	Audit Content	Resource Center	Email	Capture Leads
Blogs	Tag Content	Nurture Campaigns	Organic	Score Leads
Ebooks	Organize by Context	ABM Campaigns	Social	Drive Engagement
Infographics	Define Recommendations	Prospect Outreach	Paid Advertising	Gather Insights
Slide Decks	Build Navigation	Knowledge Base	Direct Mail	Prove ROI

Presented By Überflip

TO:

FROM:

LET'S FOCUS ON CONTENT EXPERIENCE

Made in the USA
Middletown, DE
20 January 2020

83457496R00154